WHO AM I?

A REDISCOVERY OF PURPOSE

DR. BRYAN L. MALONE, ACC

INDIE CHRISTIAN BOOK

ISBN (Paperback): 979-8-9914111-2-7

ISBN (eBook): 979-8-9914111-3-4

Library of Congress Control Number: 2024920655

Cover design by Abigail Keleher.

Published by Indie Christian Book in Bloomington, Illinois, U.S.A.

www.mgeprofessionalcoaching.com

INTRODUCTION

In late 2023, I started thinking about a resource that married men my age, forty-five, with children could utilize as they navigate life after forty. In the middle of my life, I've had many experiences that have dramatically shaped my thoughts and feelings about who I am and what I'm supposed to do with my life. These changes have often made me question whether I truly fulfill my purpose. As I continue on this personal quest, I want to connect with other men who may themselves be struggling with their identity and purpose. How is that journey going for you? Do you have tools in your toolbox to help you rediscover and redefine who you are so that you live authentically in each new stage of life? I imagine the answer is either "I'm not sure" or "No." I didn't for a long time, so I don't blame you.

As men, we go through so much and have many expectations placed on us—especially when trying to live right, be good fathers, be good husbands, or just be good people in general. In our twenties, we start trying to find our way, coming out of college or graduate school and attempting to establish a career. At that point, we're in a hurry to develop ourselves; we're not taking the time to examine who we are, familiarize ourselves with our likes and dislikes, our emotions, or the things that make us who we are. By the time we get into our forties, we're looking back on life and wondering if we somehow missed the mark. In this day and age, we are told by society to "live authentically." But how can you be authentic if you don't know who you are? Thus, this book is about the journey of *self-rediscovery:* learning who you are and defining what that means for your purpose in this stage of life.

As of writing this introduction, I've spent the past few weeks finding time every morning to connect with God. A good starting point for our mission to learn about ourselves is seeking the One Who created us. Looking at God's Word, we realize we are made in His image. If we accept this as truth and believe it, then who we are is essentially Who He is. So the question then becomes: Do we know Who He is?

The journey to self-rediscovery must start with understanding Who God is so we can live according to who He says we are. In this process, there are two levels of rediscovery at play. There's the superficial level (e.g. likes, dislikes, habits, personalities, self-care routines, etc.) and the deeper level (e.g. values, beliefs, and what makes up my core being). Understood together, these two levels provide a holistic perspective of our makeup. Once we get this picture, can we carry it forward to align the way we interact with people in public with who we are behind closed doors? Answering this question will be vital in determining whether or not you're living an authentic life.

This book will call you to take a self-inventory, incorporating resources that allow men to assess their personal and emotional makeup and biblical references that address core beliefs and values. This book will also inform you of undeniable truths about yourself, grounding your self-image in your identity in Christ. Finally, this book will coach you through discovering your purpose and fulfilling your unique calling.

Now let me preface by saying that I am not a pastor, nor do I proclaim to have life all figured out. I'm still walking my path, just like many of you, and I still make mistakes—plenty of them. So I don't speak on this subject from a place of perfection, but as someone in the struggle with you, sharing a few thoughts that have helped me along the way. The process of self-rediscovery can be long, confusing, and even uncomfortable at times, but I challenge you to stick with me until the end of this book. If you do, you may find that what makes you *you* is more powerful than you could have imagined.

CHAPTER 1

PURPOSE VS. PROFESSION

It's Monday morning and twelve days until your much-needed vacation. Lately, the weekends have become just as hurried as the weekdays, with endless errands, piles of laundry that need attention, and a house that doesn't clean or fix itself. It's one of those mornings when you feel the chill the second your toes hit the floor. You'd give anything to lay back down, pull the covers up to your chin, and get another thirty minutes of sleep, but life is calling.

You grab your keys and glance at your wife, who's already shimmying into her coat to shuttle the kids off to school. Lately, there's been a quiet distance between you, like strangers passing in the wind. A quick kiss, a downed coffee, and a handful of keys before you're in your car defrosting the windshield. That's when you glance down at your phone and see the email. Your boss has an urgent request for a presentation he needs today for the big meeting with the executives. It will be a miracle if you're home by eight.

Seven-year-old you would have been very impressed by the wool-coated professional sitting in the driver's seat. You've got a job title, a family, and a nice new sedan. You live in the suburbs in a lovely house, you have great neighbors, and the kids attend a reputable school. Life is perfect, right? Why, then, do you feel empty? What makes you so tired of the hustle and grind that you sometimes feel like leaving it all behind?

Many of us start striving from the time we're in grammar school. We want to get good grades, please our parents and teachers, and be so talented that the world can't help but notice. Such desires are often eroded as we get older and are plagued by setbacks like divorces, job layoffs, and false educational starts. These struggles leave you wondering, "What is the point of it all? Could there be some meaning beyond building a solid resume and struggling to pay the bills on time?"

It may surprise you that you can find fulfillment, no matter how old you are and how jumbled your past may seem. But you've got to start by looking up.

THE DIFFERENCE BETWEEN PROFESSION AND PURPOSE

Ask a roomful of fourth graders what the purpose of their life is, and you'll get a mosaic of answers. Many students will likely talk about their ideal professions. They want to be NBA basketball players, A-list actors, or Grammy-winning singer-songwriters. Some will talk about falling in love, getting married, and having a healthy family that will carry on their traditions. Still other students may be inclined to talk about getting rich, taking adventurous vacations, and posting about them on Instagram.

I grew up in the 80s, which was before the internet, but that didn't stop me from dreaming in color. When I was seven, I wanted to become an astronomer and spend my life studying the stars and planets. Additionally, I developed a passion for art and a talent for drawing and creating comic book stories. By the time I was a teenager, I wanted to let my creativity soar as a fashion designer. But when it was time to go to college and choose a major, I decided to become an engineer, mainly because I wanted to make a lot of money.

As most of us discover, reality often differs from what we imagined by the time we reach adulthood. I started my college career as an architectural engineering major, frequently taking classes that could cure insomnia faster than any dose of melatonin. I changed majors twice, finally settling on electronics engineering technology, mainly because six years had passed, and I needed to graduate. After graduation, I landed an engineering job that had nothing to do with what I studied in college.

Was it my dream job? Far from it, but at the time, it was what I considered a foot in the door on my journey to climb the corporate ladder of success, a path that I thought would eventually bring me happiness and fulfillment of purpose. As time passed and events unfolded, I began to question whether treading down such a path was really what I should do with my life.

Eventually, as you'll learn more about in chapter three, a transition took place. This was a good thing, because even though I was successful in my role as an engineer, I don't think it would have suited my purpose in the long term. It would have left a void in my need to positively impact others in this world. Today, I am a human resource professional for a Fortune 500 company. God has also blessed me with the opportunity to become a leadership coach, speaker, and author, and I've recently added the role of real estate investor to my portfolio. I say this not to boast of my achievements, but to illustrate the twists and turns that life can present on the road to turning our profession into purpose.

What we want to be in life regularly evolves as we age. As our responsibilities increase, we need different things and become more honest about our strengths and weaknesses. However, even as we get older and wiser, many of us may need clarification on the difference between our profession and our purpose.

Merriam-Webster's dictionary defines *profession* as "a calling requiring specialized knowledge and often long and intensive academic preparation."[1] Your profession is what you do every day to make money. You've likely gotten some education or on-the-job preparation that made you competent at what you do, which makes you a valuable resource to others who need your expertise. If you're a working adult, your profession will likely take up most of your waking hours and come with its fair share of rewards and disappointments. Yet, your profession itself isn't the source of your purpose.

The same dictionary defines *purpose* as "something set up as an object or an end to be attained."[2] In other words, your purpose is your reason for doing something. Why do you trudge away at your job, knowing your client or boss might not even be happy when you submit the proposal? You believe a payoff, or purpose, will make it worth your time. You'll earn a salary you can live on and gain valuable skills and experience that will make you a better employee. You may hope to be promoted and earn the respect of those in your household and community. Eventually, you might aspire to make more money and be able to send your kids to college without loans or buy a bigger house.

Clearly, profession is driven by purposes, but your *life's* purpose encompasses more than just your career goals. Most of us experience ups and downs that remind us that our occupation cannot be the single, lifelong pursuit that gives us meaning. No one is putting their faith in their job when they're getting a bad review. We realize that there must be something more significant to believe in.

The same holds true for our relational lives. We may start with an idealistic concept of marriage, in which our spouses will anticipate our needs, comfort us in our failures, and always look and smell great. The reality is something different. Our spouses are fragile humans who need things from us, too. Men, for example, are often

---

1. *Merriam-Webster Dictionary*, s.v. "profession (*n.*)," accessed March 12, 2024, https://www.merriam-webster.com/dictionary/profession.
2. *Merriam-Webster Dictionary*, s.v. "purpose (*n.*)," accessed March 12, 2024, https://www.merriam-webster.com/dictionary/purpose.

keenly aware that our wives need us for financial support and emotional strength. This burden drives us to "crush it" at work and seem confident, no matter what happens to us personally. However, to be that driven and accomplished person in the workplace, we first need to know that we are unconditionally respected and loved at home.

An ultimate purpose for life helps bring all the foggy pieces of one's past together. We can handle setbacks, toil away, and treat our spouses properly as long as there is a payoff, a worthwhile reason for doing it all.

Many people create this purpose out of money, believing their lives will be problem-free once they can pay off their car or buy a second home. Others find their goal in romance, always looking to attract a perfect mate who will bring them layers of happiness. Still others strive for status, thinking fulfillment will come once someone calls them "doctor" or "attorney," or they have a C-suite title behind their name.

Unfortunately, many discover too late that these prizes, while nice to have, can never honestly fill their hearts. We can all name plenty of celebrities who have opulent homes, classy wardrobes, and all the notoriety they could wish for yet have life-threatening problems with drugs or alcohol. Famous folks like Elizabeth Taylor have married up to eight times without ever finding the lifelong bliss that romance promised them. And many individuals succeed in earning the titles they spent years studying for, only to realize that they still struggle with the same sense of self-doubt.

The reality is that the only purpose that can motivate us and last for all eternity comes from a Higher Being. Before anything else, we must know that we are loved unconditionally and valued immensely. Then, we can start pursuing the surface-level wins with conviction. I have spent much of my life hoping, planning, and making mistakes, all while putting my faith in the wrong things. Material possessions and other superficial goals, while nice to achieve, did not bring true fulfillment. Eventually, I learned to trust that God has a plan for my life. And I believe He has a plan for your life as well. Once you seek His purpose for your life, your profession, personal goals, and relational life will fall in line.

GOD AND PURPOSE

The world loves to pigeonhole us. Our marital status, profession, and even number of children shuffle us into different categories. Advertisers sell us their wares based on these identities, and we often choose our friends because of the external factors we have in common.

God, however, uses a different scale to evaluate us. To Him, our value is based on the perfect holiness of His Son, Jesus. In Him, we are redeemed, victorious, and set apart. We could never earn this status, but luckily, we don't have to; it is a free gift of grace.

Once we understand who we are on a deeper level, we don't have to prove ourselves on the surface. We don't have to compare our circumstances to our peers' or be ashamed that our lives didn't turn out as planned when we were young. However, our heavenly Father requires that we fill our minds and days with pure, lovely, and excellent things (Philippians 4:8). We cannot simply sit back and eat Cheetos, watch bad videos, and wait until the second coming. Neither can we be distracted by doing too many things unrelated to our purpose. We have to be diligent and intentional about living out our purpose, which ultimately brings God glory.

We all have personalities, talents, and experiences that make us best suited to various professions and ministries, all of which have been gifted to us to bring glory to God. This book will help you uncover your gifts and personality traits, the things that make you *you*. Beyond that, it will help you rediscover your identity in Christ, which will make background noise out of all the opinions the world loves to throw at us. I look forward to taking this journey together!

QUESTIONS

1. What did you want to be when you were in elementary school? How about in high school or college? Did you end up fulfilling your original dream or taking another path?
2. How do you use your talents and skills in your current line of work? Are there other gifts you could be employing but don't have an outlet for?
3. How do you think the world defines your worth? How do you think God does? Which one of these is more important, and why?

CHAPTER 2
GOD'S PURPOSE VS. OURS

I f you've ever given your kids an allowance, you know how important having a clear purpose is. As an adult, you've learned that the best use of the money they earn would be to save some of it for something they can enjoy long-term, or at least more than once. Young children, however, have different ideas. Their purpose is often to purchase candy or fast food that will be gone by dinnertime. Eventually, many children learn the value of saving because they no longer wish to see their precious income disappear immediately.

In the same way, we can often misinterpret the purpose of our lives. Many believe they are here to make money, build an impressive career, or get elected to public office. There's nothing wrong with these goals, but they aren't God's ultimate purpose for our time on earth.

GOD'S PURPOSE FOR US

When we stand before God to give an account of our lives, He will not ask about our bank statements, waist sizes, or Facebook profiles.

He won't even ask about the "good deeds" we did while on earth. Instead, He'll ask what we did to serve Him and honor Him. Did we use our gifts and talents to serve others? Did we help draw others into a relationship with Him?

Many of us begin our careers in fields that do not suit our talents or bring Him glory. This is because we seek not God's will but our own. Developing a vital relationship with the Lord early in life can save you a lot of heartache in the long run. I got saved at age nine. However, I didn't discover my purpose until I was thirty-eight years old. This was part of God's plan, and even though I wish it happened sooner, I'm glad I found it when I did. It's never too late to discover God's true calling in your life.

Many do not seek God's purpose because they feel unworthy. "If you knew what I've done, Bryan," you may be thinking, "and the things I think about, you would not be telling me that I am loved by God." Believe me, I know what that feels like; I've had those thoughts myself. But you'll be relieved to know that His love for us is based not on our goodness, but on the perfection and sacrifice of Jesus Christ. He knew our weaknesses when He called us, and He wasn't worried about them. When God isn't stressed about something, that's a good sign we don't need to be, either.

In John 15:16, Jesus tells us, "You did not choose me, but I chose you and appointed you so that you might go and bear fruit—fruit that will last—and so that whatever you ask in my name the Father will give you." God has hand-picked us for a relationship with Him so that we will bear beautiful fruit that the whole world can celebrate! If we want to find our purpose, it's vital to grow in knowing Him first. Talk to God in prayer, read scriptures, and meditate on them. This will be the light that guides you and the fuel that moves you through a life of ups and downs.

God's Word teaches us what it means to live in happiness that renews daily. Galatians 5:22-23 tells us, "But the fruit of the Spirit is love, joy, peace, forbearance, kindness, goodness, faithfulness, gentleness and self-control. Against such things there is no law."

When we live in the Spirit, we'll exhibit the love, joy, peace, and patience the world desperately needs to see.

If you've been around for any length of time, you know that people excel at different things. For example, you might know someone who is exceptionally patient or exhibits remarkable self-control. These traits take years to acquire for some, while certain gifts come more naturally to others.

In addition, some people have talents that you don't. For example, some Christians are good with numbers, administration, or working with youth. Others may have gifts of the Holy Spirit, such as discernment, that you admire. God gives us spiritual gifts, natural talents, and personality traits that make us best suited for different ministries. These are critical to our purpose here on earth. In chapters five and six, we'll delve deeper into discovering your practical purpose.

OUR IDENTITY IN CHRIST

Before you know your purpose, you've got to be grounded in your identity in Christ. The dictionary defines *identity* as "the distinguishing character or personality of an individual."[1] People are so eager for identity these days that they will alter their dress, profession, or even their gender to have a distinguishing quality.

We all get a degree of identity from our earthly pursuits. You might say, "I am a doctor," "I am a father of three," or "I am an American." We are letting others know what we do with our time and what is important to us. However, our identity in Christ won't change if we move or our kids attend college. It is something that no one can take away.

The world, the enemy, and our inner voices often play tricks on

---

1. *Merriam-Webster Dictionary*, s.v. "identity (*n.*)," accessed July 11, 2024, https://www.merriam-webster.com/dictionary/identity.

us. They will tell us that we are lazy, useless, or not good enough. But Jesus tells us something different.

First of all, you must know that if you're in Christ, you are *redeemed*. While sin is in our nature, our Savior does not see us as hopeless sinners. Ephesians 1:7 says, "In him we have redemption through his blood, the forgiveness of sins, in accordance with the riches of God's grace." When God looks at us, He sees the righteousness of His Son, which makes us wholly acceptable to Him.

Secondly, *God loves you immensely*. Many of us grew up in church singing songs about God's love, yet we have never let the truth of this reality sink in. The God of the Universe, Who created all the scenery we admire and the excellent characteristics we notice in others, loves us more than we could know!

Romans 8:38-39 tells us,

[38] For I am convinced that neither death nor life, neither angels nor demons, neither the present nor the future, nor any powers, [39] neither height nor depth, nor anything else in all creation, will be able to separate us from the love of God that is in Christ Jesus our Lord.

Many of us have experienced the loss of a loved one, a career, or a marriage. But the love of God is something that no one and nothing can take away from us, no matter what we lose here on earth. That is something worthy of our praise.

Galatians 2:20 tells us, "I have been crucified with Christ and I no longer live, but Christ lives in me. The life I now live in the body, I live by faith in the Son of God, who loved me and gave himself for me." Since Christ lives in me, I can live by faith in Him and His love for me.

Thirdly, God calls us *powerful, courageous, and disciplined*. Many of us have never thought of ourselves as remarkably disciplined or brave—myself included! We know we tend to be lazy and shy away from conflict. Yet 2 Timothy 1:7 says, "For the Spirit God gave us does not make us timid, but gives us power, love and self-discipline." If the Spirit of God is in you, you can be bold, strong, and sacrificial. You can work hard at your job, even when you don't feel like it, and stand up for what is right. As believers in Christ, we don't need to fear the opinions of men. God gives us strength when the time is right.

Fourthly, *we are supported and cared for*. Psalm 37:25 says, "I was young and now I am old, yet I have never seen the righteous forsaken or their children begging bread." As children of God, He will supply our needs. He will give us the food, clothing, and shelter we need to live and help the hurting. We don't have to worry about who will look after us or where our resources will come from. We have a good Father Who will provide, even when we mess up.

Fifthly, He calls us *generous*. Psalm 37:26 says of the righteous, "They are always generous and lend freely; their children will be a blessing." A generous person is willing to give their time and money to help others and is an excellent witness of God's love for the world. If you're a family man, generosity will go a long way toward earning the respect of those in your household. Being generous does not require you to be rich first. When you are generous, you work hard and freely share the fruits of your labor, ensuring that those in your family and beyond are appropriately cared for. Your children will notice and be a blessing to the world in turn.

The sixth part of our identity is *victory*. Most of us know what it's like to have enemies. These people may be in our schools, places of work, or even in our communities. They criticize, gossip, manipulate, and may even lie on you just to get ahead. Yet God gives us the ultimate victory. Through Him, we have peace, righteousness, security, and triumph over the opposition—making our enemies our footstool (Psalm 110:1).

Isaiah 54:17 says, "'No weapon forged against you will prevail, and you will refute every tongue that accuses you. This is the heritage of the servants of the Lord, and this is their vindication from me,' declares the Lord." Many may accuse you and seek to destroy your character, yet God will ultimately defeat all of them. We shouldn't be afraid because of the fact that many live as enemies of the cross (Philippians 3:18). Rather, we can walk in victory, knowing that we are children of the light and our Father is more significant than any person or spirit in the world. We will see Him win.

Seventh, our identity is as one *fearfully and wonderfully made* (Psalm 139:14). In these days of advertisements and social media posts featuring flawless bodies, teeth, and outfits (most of which are photoshopped), it's easy for average folks to cancel themselves out as undesirable. Yet that is not what God says about you. He formed us in our mothers' wombs, knowing our purpose before we could even crawl (Jeremiah 1:5). God made us with care and reverence. We are worth more than many sparrows to Him (Matthew 10:31). The very number of the hairs on our heads is known to Him (Luke 12:7). Therefore, we can be proud of our bodies, faces, and identities. Every detail is exactly as God wants it to be.

Psalm 119:73 says, "Your hands made me and formed me; give me understanding to learn your commands." God created us by His own hands, and He calls us to learn and follow His Word.

The eighth part of our identity is that we were *chosen and set apart.* 1 Peter 2:9 says, "But you are a chosen people, a royal priesthood, a holy nation, God's special possession, that you may declare the praises of him who called you out of darkness into his wonderful light." God has called you and I to be a part of a chosen people, set apart to dwell in the light and live a holy life. He has selected His people to obey, residing in His special way so that we might sing His praises. That is an identity worth living for!

Finally, *God called you before you were born, consecrating you* (Jeremiah 1:5). He called Jeremiah to be a prophet, but He may have called you to be a teacher, a parent, or a scientist. He knew all of this before you were born. If you ever feel unworthy, know that you're not alone. But understand that your purpose is not something you dreamed up, and feelings of inadequacy or low self-worth do not negate your purpose. God designated it before the beginning of time.

Life can often cause us to take our eyes off the way our Father sees us. Yet God's value on us should be the foundation of our identity. Many say they base their values on their faith, which is a good starting point. But the most crucial element is who we are in His eyes. Our faith is where we go when we feel lost, purposeless, or tired. Our minds will be renewed once we see who we are in Him. There is a significant reason for everything we do, and we need to be reminded of it often.

LOST IDENTITY

Many of us begin our walks with Christ with great passion. But over time, the distractions and worries of this life leave us feeling alone and defeated.

The further we are from God, the more likely we will lose awareness of our identity in Him. The good news is that, though we may temporarily lose our way, we haven't lost our identity outright. Our faith may sometimes weaken, but that doesn't mean God has left us.

Rediscovery is all about reconnection. We need to get in touch and open our eyes. What we have been looking for in all the wrong places has been in front of us the whole time. You can read many Christian books and devotionals (just like this one) that help explain your purpose in Christ, but no one can reach out and reconnect for you. Use these resources to inspire your journey of rediscovery of identity and purpose through Jesus. Will you do this today?

QUESTIONS

1. What are some ways in which you usually identify yourself? How do they fail to give the whole picture of who you are?
2. How do you feel your role in your profession or family ties in with God's larger purpose for your life?

3. When are some times when you need to be reminded of your identity in Him? Which aspects of this identity do you need to hear the most often, and why?
4. How is your identity in Christ a foundation for the way you live your life?

CHAPTER 3
CONTENTMENT VS. REGRET

As I write this book in early 2024, at age forty-five, I have often struggled with discontentment. I have thought that, by now, I should have achieved a particular leadership position at my job. Or, I should be further along in retirement savings than I am. Or, I'm not making the money I should be making to give my family the comfortable lifestyle I desire for them to have.

I've even gone so far as to question decisions that I made as early as my senior year of high school, when I decided to stay home and go to college rather than leave my hometown of Memphis, a choice that ultimately came down to a lack of financial aid. I think about what my life would have been like had I been able to venture out and live in another city, another state, or a different part of the country. Without proper perspective to put them in check, all of these ideas have swirled around my head and caused me to question whether I'm where I'm supposed to be at this point in my life.

Social media doesn't help in this downward spiral of "I wish I had just..." We see peers from our school days who started families younger, majored in something more lucrative, or still have all their hair and are in great shape, and we begin to wish we had chosen differently. We think our lives would be excellent if we had just taken a more imaginative turn when the road forked. This questioning and speculation can cause us to mentally check out, missing opportunities for growth and fulfillment and failing to consider the purpose God has for us in the present.

The truth is that we all make trade-offs when we opt to take one path over another. That person with older children may have struggled financially during their twenties and thirties. The wealthy businessperson may rarely see their family. Those ultra-attractive folks may not be fulfilled vocationally. We are only looking at one part of the story. Some people probably check out my profile and say, "I wish I had Bryan's career and family. Then my life would be perfect."

Contentment, however, is something we learn. We can make the choice to be happy where we are and with the people in our lives, or we can spend our time longing for a life we cannot have. In reality, if we had a time machine and could go back in time and make different choices, we would just have different regrets. At some point, we must learn the art of accepting life's imperfections and becoming content where we are. Only then will we have the focus we need to pursue our purpose.

Contentment is a key ingredient to rediscovering purpose. It allows us to focus on what lies ahead, not on what is behind us. See, friend, purpose is forward-looking. It has to do with what lies in front of you. You find the road ahead by looking through the windshield, not at something you think you see in the rear-view mirror.

When you are content, you can look at your current situation and know that you are precisely where God wants you to be in this season of your life. This is not to say that the situation will last forever, but you are in this season for a reason. There is something God expects you to learn and grow from as a result. Contentment keeps our hearts in the right place when reconnecting with our purpose. For example, if my purpose is to inspire others and help them become the best version of themselves, I must first be content with who I am, where I am in life, and what I have before I can be of any help to them.

The key to contentment is knowing who we are in our heavenly Father. We are created in His image, but what qualifies us for a close relationship with Him is our Savior, Jesus. The secret to reconnecting with Him is to remind ourselves daily of the standing we have with Him thanks to Christ's redeeming work. He died for our sins so we can be sons of the Great King. Through His Word, we discover what true happiness looks like again. We refocus on what genuinely matters. We can live our lives in gratitude for what He has blessed us with, rather than in a state of complaining about what we don't have.

If all I feel is regret, I will act out in dangerous ways. I may become a greedy workaholic, looking for money and an opulent lifestyle to prove myself to the world. Or I may give in to low self-esteem, spending my days on the couch, binge watching mind-numbing TV, and wondering what went wrong. But if other people depend on me and I have an essential role in my world, I must rise above those proclivities. I've got to be at my best and confidently look toward the future if I want to help others. This requires a healthy, content outlook.

FEDEX, THE APOSTLE PAUL, AND CONTENTMENT

In 2018, I got promoted to management at FedEx. I had high hopes for moving up in the company and thought I could become a vice president one day. That all changed when I learned about a "voluntary company buyout," the corporation's way of reducing the number of employees without actually laying anyone off. At the time, I was managing a small team of eight professionals. It was disbanded, and my employees were reassigned, with one taking the buyout. I became concerned about my future there for the first time in my more than twenty-five years with the company.

The change made me question my loyalty to the company and its loyalty to me. I began considering the possibility of life after FedEx, and I started doing a lot of soul-searching. I watched YouTube videos and sought the wisdom of gurus like Dr. Myles Munroe, Les Brown, and Dr. Eric Thomas. I have never met any of them, but they walked me through a tough patch in my life.

Problems can be valuable if we learn from them. If it hadn't been for FedEx's downsizing, I never would have discovered the fulfilling career path I am on now. The same is true with many failures and setbacks. God may simply be redirecting us to something better. You could end up being the Dr. Myles Munroe in someone else's life, helping them to their feet because you know what it's like to have fallen on the same sidewalk.

Life offers no shortage of disappointments. Not long into adulthood, we will discover that the things we often put our hopes in will disappoint us. Friends will gossip about us, our jobs can be tedious, and spouses don't always provide us with the perfect encouragement. God is teaching us to mature, and we must learn to put our faith in Him alone. That's something we can't lose.

In the book of Philippians, the Apostle Paul told us about contentment.

> [11] I am not saying this because I am in need, for I have learned to be content whatever the circumstances. [12] I know what it is to be in need, and I know what it is to have plenty. I have learned the secret of being content in any and every situation, whether well-fed or hungry, whether living in plenty or in want. [13] I can do all this through him who gives me strength. (Philippians 4:11-13)

Paul knew what it was like to be rich, and he also understood poverty. He was shipwrecked, imprisoned, beaten, and hungry. And you think you've got it rough! Paul would have been decimated by despair if he hadn't learned that contentment comes from above. We can all find things to cry about. Still, when we turn to Jesus, we find a peace that doesn't change with the stock market.

Paul reminds us that the secret to contentment is that "I can do all things through Him who gives me strength." Contentment lets us focus on what is ahead of us rather than what is in the past. You can accept your season of life for what it is and create new goals for yourself. When you were younger, you made decisions based on what seemed right according to your limited understanding. Now, you can plan for the future based on your newfound maturity. Most of all, you're better prepared to make decisions now, because God, the most powerful One in the universe, is the Person giving you strength.

Note that there is nothing wrong with having goals and wanting to improve yourself or the situation around you. But contentment keeps our hearts from giving way to greed, covetousness, low self-esteem, and other factors that do not serve us when trying to reconnect with our purpose. Gratefulness is equally crucial and will be discussed later.

HOW TO FIND CONTENTMENT

Some people fear contentment because they confuse it with complacency, which occurs when one refuses to be aware of the problems and challenges around them. Complacent people are often glib and foolish, always joking around and never getting to business. However, you won't lose your drive to succeed if you are content with what you have. You just have to be honest about where you are and where you'd like to be one, five, or even ten years from now.

You might be thinking, "Hey, Bryan, that sounds excellent. But I've been restless and unhappy for many years. How do I change my mindset?"

Well, you won't change overnight, but there are things you can do right now to start the upward spiral. Eventually, you will learn to take every thought captive (2 Corinthians 10:5). When you find yourself staring at an old classmate's social media profile or spending too much time imagining your life with a different spouse, stop. Remember the things you have that others only dream about. Do you have your health? Did you wake up with air in your lungs and all four limbs? Do you have a family? Can you pay the bills? Then you're doing a lot better than many. Learn to view yourself as a blessed person rather than a victim of your choices.

Lately, gratitude journaling has gained popularity. In this practice, you discipline yourself to write down things you're grateful for daily. Your gratitude journal could be a physical journal you keep by your bedside or an electronic document where you jot things down a few times a week. Many journals are specifically designed for gratitude reflections; some will even prompt you. If you're a visual thinker, like I am, you can purchase a journal that allows you to include drawings or graphs. Many folks like to keep their reflections between themselves and God, but some people like to share their discoveries and allow others to chime in with their insights. If this is you, a blog or website may be the proper format.

It's essential to keep your journal specific. Sometimes, we say things like "I'm grateful for my family," or "I have a roof over my head" without going into enough detail for the significance of those blessings to sink in. Instead, you can write things like "I'm thrilled my daughter wants to try out for the school play," or "praise God that we were able to pay the plumber." This will also help boost your confidence, reminding you that you're doing many things right.

In addition, you'll want to journal about small triumphs that are an improvement over your past. For example, you may be learning to control your emotions better when you have discipline. Write down all the times you took a deep breath instead of saying something hurtful to your kids in a moment of anger. Maybe you could never afford to buy a car, and you're finally able to. Writing down victories like this may keep you from dreaming about "the good ol' days" when you were younger (but not better looking!). Even if you could go back in time, you would realize that things were not as carefree as you remember. You're learning and growing every day, and that's something to be grateful for.

If you're like most grown-ups, you'll have some "A-plus" days, where the right opportunities pop up like crocuses and your kids behave like angels. There will also be days when everything you touch falls to pieces. It helps to write about the specks of hope you experienced during these challenging times. Maybe you got a compliment from a supervisor or had no cavities at the dentist. This will keep you from ruminating about your problems. Instead, you can be grateful for small things and begin the following day without a cloud over your head. There's a chance your concerns will have already started to work themselves out anyway.

Another way to foster contentment is to spend time with those you love and do things that bring you joy. As a hard-working professional and parent, I know how scarce time can be. Sometimes, the easiest thing to do after a long day of meetings, traffic, pickups, drop-offs, helping with homework, and preparing dinner is to collapse on the couch and tune everyone else out. However, that may not be the best medicine for your soul. Try to find time each day to read an exciting book or take a walk outside. Call someone who makes you laugh. Join a club for people who like to play golf or cook as much as you do. Once you begin enjoying your life, you'll have less time to think about how it's let you down.

Taking care of your physical health will also help your mental state. This doesn't mean you need to diet constantly or subject yourself to intense workouts every morning. It does, however, mean being careful about what you eat and getting some movement every day. You might enjoy a gentle walk or a workout video you can do in the morning before work. Committing to this discipline may seem tiring initially, but it will ultimately help you in all your work. Endorphins relieve stress and make you feel better about yourself. The confidence you gain from completing the physical challenge will also improve the way others see you. I have had a regular exercise routine since college, which has helped me remain resilient through many setbacks and challenges. As one imperfect man to another, I can tell you it's worth it to get the ball rolling.

THE BENEFITS OF CONTENTMENT

As you write down your grateful thoughts, you'll begin to dwell on the positive aspects of your life. This will do more than make you more positive, and it will give you a host of benefits aside from allowing you to hone in on your purpose. A content outlook is essential to your mental and physical well-being.

Focusing on what you're grateful for will make you happier. Physically, this can help lower your risk of high blood pressure, heart attack, and stroke. You'll also be less tempted to stress-eat, a problem that can cause several serious health issues. Happiness will also help you to sleep better and have an easier time being active, which will further improve your physical health.[1]

Furthermore, being content will improve your relationships. We all know how we treat our spouses after beating ourselves up all day. A negative self-perception results in a short temper and insecurity, neither of which will help you be a solid partner. A grateful mindset will make you someone others trust. You may even find them confiding in you about their problems because they admire your peace.

A content individual will also be a better employee. When you don't feel bad about past decisions or wish you could have a different life, you can focus on the tasks you're given with a cheerful attitude. Of course, this will make you someone your supervisors notice, and you may even get promoted. Yet even if they don't reward you, you can be happy knowing you're doing your best at the job God has assigned you.

Being a better parent, friend, spouse, and employee will improve your health and your external life and make you more content on the inside. Refusing to live with negative thoughts can spark a healthy

---

1. "How Happiness Affects Health," www.heart.org, May 20, 2020, https://www.heart.org/en/university-hospitals-harrington-heart-and-vascular/how-happiness-affects-health.

bonfire of positivity in your life. Be sure to thank God every day for His blessings. In doing so, you'll free your heart and mind to see the purpose He has in store for you.

QUESTIONS

1. What are some activities that make you content? How can you incorporate these into your life more?
2. What blessings do you often take for granted in your life? How can you remind yourself to be grateful for them?
3. What type of gratitude journal appeals to you? How could this practice help make you a better employee or parent?

CHAPTER 4

LONELINESS VS. CONNECTION

I n October 2016, I traveled to Belgium for the very first time. I had traveled internationally before, but it was my first trip to Europe. I was there on official FedEx business (shout out to Fred Smith for sponsoring the opportunity). We had just acquired TNT, and I was on the project team that was responsible for coordinating the first ever flight from Liege to Memphis. For the first visit, I was there for two weeks (I would travel there three more times over the course of six months).

Overall, the experience was phenomenal. The first week was filled with meetings, and on the weekend, I got a chance to visit several historical landmarks. But I began to miss my family. By the time the second week rolled around, I was feverishly counting the days until I would head back home. It was obvious that despite the excitement of traveling abroad, loneliness had set in. After a while, I began dreading the long two-week stints away from home, the eight-hour flights, and living out of hotels. How many of you have had a similar experience that caused loneliness to creep in?

Loneliness can completely rob us of our joy, especially when part of our purpose is to have a family. Dating sites and singles' bars are full of people looking to escape the trials of flying solo. However, we also know folks who remain lonely in a healthy-looking team. They have a family, church leaders, friends, and coworkers who all seem supportive, yet these folks still feel misunderstood and often believe they are navigating life alone.

Could it be that we haven't genuinely experienced grace and gratitude in our hearts? Is that the reason for loneliness in the presence of good company? Moreover, what is wrong with feeling lonely? Isn't loneliness just one more negative feeling we have to learn to keep under control? Let's explore these questions further.

THE PROBLEM WITH LONELINESS

Now, you may be thinking: "Bryan, I understand the connection between being content and rediscovering my purpose, but is the problem of loneliness really relevant here?" Simply put, yes, it is. In life, many things will distract you from your purpose. But if the pursuit of purpose is like swimming across a sea, unchecked loneliness is like the tide that pulls you back, preventing your progress and even threatening to pull you under. A good community, however, can be the inflatable inner tube that helps you coast when you're ready to give up.

We all experience a hodgepodge of emotions throughout the day, but loneliness comes with a unique set of dangers. A study from the *Archives of Internal Medicine* found that 43% of older adults report feelings of loneliness. The study also found that loneliness increased the risk of death and loss of functionality.[1]

In 2017, U.S. Surgeon General Vivek Murthy concluded that "loneliness and weak social connections are associated with a reduction in lifespan similar to that caused by smoking 15 cigarettes a day

---

1. Carla M. Perissinotto, Irena Stijacic Cenzer, and Kenneth E. Covinsky, "Loneliness in Older Persons: A Predictor of Functional Decline and Death," *Archives of Internal Medicine* 172, no. 14 (July 23, 2012), https://doi.org/10.1001/archinternmed.2012.1993.

and even greater than that associated with obesity."[2] In other words, feeling lonely can reduce your life expectancy even more than being overweight or smoking.

Loneliness can increase your chances of hospitalization or death from heart failure by 15%-20%, but only if you *feel* lonely.[3] Some people may live alone without feelings of isolation or despair. If you are happily single, by all means, keep doing your thing! Yet it remains clear that many people suffer from loneliness, and it's a detriment to their physical and emotional well-being.

Studies show that loneliness impacts certain groups more than others, including young adults, older adults, adults living alone, and low-income adults. These individuals are also at a greater risk for psychological issues, such as depression, addiction, and self-harm.[4]

Loneliness can be the result of a downward spiral. Folks may isolate themselves due to past hurt, social anxiety, or low self-esteem and discover that being alone makes their troubles even worse. They give in to feelings of despair and find themselves increasingly hurt, awkward, and afraid of being social.

As you can see, loneliness takes a toll. The effects of loneliness can be crippling to the journey of self-rediscovery and the fulfillment of purpose. When we're battling loneliness, not only are we potentially lacking a critical support system, including mentors, prayer partners, and like-minded people whose purposes align with ours, but we're often demotivated and unconfident in ourselves and our goals. If we're going to figure out who we are and what we're made for, combating loneliness needs to be one of our first steps.

---

2. Vivek Murthy, "Work and the Loneliness Epidemic," Harvard Business Review, September 26, 2017, https://hbr.org/2017/09/work-and-the-loneliness-epidemic.

3. Sam Roth, "Social Isolation, Loneliness Increase Risk for Heart Failure," American College of Cardiology, February 1, 2023, https://www.acc.org/About-ACC/Press-Releases/2023/02/01/21/26/Social-Isolation-Loneliness-Increase-Risk-for-Heart-Failure#:

4. "Health Effects of Social Isolation and Loneliness," Centers for Disease Control and Prevention, March 26, 2024, https://www.cdc.gov/social-connectedness/risk-factors/index.html.

THE CURE

If you don't have a lot of practice being social, you might be feeling intimidated, but getting out of your shell and seeking connection may be easier than you think. You can start small by joining a club or online group and interacting only when you feel comfortable. If you have a close relative or friend you can trust, call them and talk for ten minutes. They will probably be happy to hear from you!

These interactions can give you the confidence to speak to others you don't know as well. You can begin with superficial conversations about the weather or your favorite musicians. Once you develop trust, you can share more personal matters with others.

Maybe you've experienced loss or rejection that has caused you to shy away from connections. Serving others is a great way to get your mind off yourself and onto those in need. Could you tutor or mentor a struggling teen once a week? Can you listen to the fascinating stories of an older person in an assisted living facility? Could you dedicate your time to serving at your local church in some capacity?

These activities seem draining on the surface, but participating in them can energize you. While showing empathy for someone else, you'll forget your own disappointments. It may also help you appreciate your situation more.

Pastor Jetezen Franklin spoke about the need to share love, even when we have been hurt.[5] God continues to love us through our messes, and we must show that same grace and unrelenting love toward others. Jesus commands us to do so in scriptures like Galatians 6:2, which tells us: "Carry each other's burdens, and in this way you will fulfill the law of Christ." God tells us to look at the hardships that plague others and find ways to help ease their loads. When we

---

5. Jentezen Franklin, "Love Like You've Never Been Hurt," Jentezen Franklin (Blog), April 13, 2018, https://jentezenfranklin.org/blog/love-like-youve-never-been-hurt/.

serve, a sense of gratitude and fulfillment will eat away at feelings of loneliness until we forget they're there.

If you're sensitive, it's essential to focus on what others need and not what they might say about you when you're gone. Concern for the opinions of idle people is a surefire way to become frustrated and depressed.

The gratefulness discussed in the previous chapter is also critical to combating loneliness. Many of us spend our social time comparing ourselves to others, which could make talking and sharing incredibly painful. If you do this, you will likely feel that you don't measure up, since we all have different strengths and weaknesses. But if you're counting your blessings, you won't waste time on comparisons. Instead, you can concentrate on loving and meeting the needs of the person God has placed in front of you.

LONELY WITH COMPANY

I also want to address the needs of those who are "lonely with company." These are people who connect with others regularly but still feel alone. In these cases, the problem may be a spiritual one. No matter how understanding and warm your friends and church associations may be, you'll never experience complete grace and love from them. That's because God is the only One Who can thoroughly heal us.

If you feel lonely despite an active social life, I encourage you to dig deeper into your relationship with your Savior. Write things down in a journal if it helps. What sins has He forgiven you, and what spiritual gifts has He bestowed? Do you believe that His grace covers everything? If so, you are genuinely saved and never alone. God knows you better than you know yourself, and He loves you anyway. That assurance will not leave you empty, seeking to fill your heart with approval from people. It will fill you up and make you satisfied.

If necessary, enlist the help of a Christian counselor in your journey. Join a Bible study and carefully pursue a meaningful relationship with your Savior. Read Christian books or listen to podcasts during your commute. Don't give up until the reality of grace and truth has sunk deep into your soul.

THE BENEFITS OF CONNECTION

Many of us automatically think of romantic relationships when we consider connections. However, there are many ways to be close to those we aren't dating or married to. For example, you may want to take your kids out for ice cream and discuss what matters to them. You could join a local club or community group. Or you could simply force yourself to talk to a few people on your way to your cubicle in the morning. Even if your interactions are superficial, you may find yourself immediately experiencing a lifted mood. This is the magic of human connection.

According to Stanford University, well-connected people enjoy a 50% increased chance of longevity and an improved immune system.[6] The right connections will also increase your self-esteem and empathy for others. As you listen more, you'll become an even stronger friend, leading to even more connections. Those who are well-socialized are also at a lower risk for anxiety and depression. This is a real blessing, because if left untreated, these common mental health issues can lead to more serious ones.

There is also evidence that connecting with others can help you maintain a healthy body mass index, improve cancer survival, decrease cardiovascular mortality, and increase overall mental health.[7] None of us will enjoy perfect health every day. When you

---

6. Emma Seppälä, "Connectedness & Health: The Science of Social Connection," The Center for Compassion and Altruism Research and Education, May 8, 2014, https://ccare.stanford.edu/uncategorized/connectedness-health-the-science-of-social-connection-infographic/.

7. Jessica Martino, Jennifer Pegg, and Elizabeth Pegg Frates, "The Connection Prescription: Using the Power of Social Interactions and the Deep Desire for Connect-

aren't in peak form, existing close connections can help you get back to where you want to be, physically and mentally.

At some level, you must interact with others if you want a long, happy, healthy life (I know some introverts may disagree with me on this, and that's okay). But beyond that, you must find trustworthy people with whom to share your hopes and fears, which can ease the burden on your soul and help you see clearly when you're overwhelmed. You may even find yourself strong enough to be a rock for someone else when they need a listening ear.

DROPPING THE BITTERNESS

Unfortunately, past hurts hold many folks back from experiencing the benefits of social connection. If you cling to the pain long enough, it will eventually become a numbing bitterness. You won't want to connect with others because things they say will remind you of unhealed pain. And the isolation that results will continue to make you less likable.

Some people can't move on with healthy relationships because of mistreatment by relatives, peer groups, or even church members in the past. But instead of protecting themselves, they end up only hurting themselves by their lack of forgiveness. Holding onto the offense won't do anything to punish your offender, who may not even be aware that you're still angry.

It's possible to move past the hulking boulder of past hurt, but you may need to enlist the help of a professional. A pastor or therapist can do wonders to help you peel back the layers so you can move forward.

Often, it helps to know that you don't have to trust those who hurt you; you only need to forgive them. This forgiveness allows you to become more like your Savior, Who forgot your sins and tossed

edness to Empower Health and Wellness," *American Journal of Lifestyle Medicine* 11, no. 6 (October 7, 2015): 466–75, https://doi.org/10.1177/1559827615608788.

them into the depths of the sea (Micah 7:19). Letting go of past pain is necessary for you to move forward in faith (Matthew 5:23-24) and to form meaningful relationships with others.

CONNECTING IN MIDLIFE

Unlike younger individuals, those of us approaching or experiencing midlife (45-64 years old) have unique challenges when it comes to connecting. We may have less leisure time due to the demands of work, family, or aging parents. It's unlikely that we'll be "going out" all night on the weekends, looking for people to grab a drink with or companions for an impromptu getaway trip. Furthermore, our problems and decisions might affect more people as we age. We need to make connections with those who are taking life seriously. And many of us, especially men, need to maintain the respect of those in our community, even while we face life's struggles.

Social media may compound these issues, because it's easier for some to hide behind a screen persona and have superficial interactions than to talk face-to-face, especially when pressed for time. However, in-person interactions have been shown to create a more significant mood boost than those happening online.[8]

Making midlife friends could be as simple as taking a class in something that interests you, such as woodworking or cycling. These skills will also help keep your mind and body sharp. If your ultimate goal is to form connections, commit to talking with at least one person a week. Remember that those whose company you enjoy most may be older or younger than you. That's okay, as long as your interactions lift you and help you feel fulfilled.

Christians will eventually want to form bonds on a deeper level. The writer of Hebrews tells us in chapter ten to "not giv[e] up

---

8. Gwendolyn Seidman, "How Do Digital and In-Person Interactions Affect Wellbeing?" Psychology Today, September 6, 2022, https://www.psychologytoday.com/us/blog/close-encounters/202209/how-do-digital-and-in-person-interactions-affect-wellbeing.

meeting together, as some are in the habit of doing, but encourag[e] one another—and all the more as you see the Day approaching" (verse 25). When you're in a crisis or facing temptation, you'll need other believers to lift you up and encourage you. You won't want folks simply giving you feel-good advice that will lead you down a messy path. Instead, you'll need brothers and sisters who will tell the truth in love and remind you of God's purpose for you.

Many churches, especially larger ones, use a "small group" model that matches folks based on their ages, neighborhoods, or interests. Some small groups study the Bible together and share insights and discoveries. Most also have a prayer time, during which you can share your needs and praises from the week. Some simply meet up at coffee shops, restaurants, or in the comfort of a living room just to fellowship. Small groups are great places to make connections, form Godly relationships, and do life with fellow believers within the local church, which is its designed intent.

As you connect, you'll find people you admire and others who seek to emulate your best qualities. Connection allows you to build each other up, even when you aren't explicitly speaking words of encouragement over each other. Furthermore, serving and making a difference in your church and community can lead to leadership opportunities. Being in your midlife gives you an excellent platform from which to share your lessons with those who need to hear them.

Your age doesn't determine your ability to form meaningful friendships. It can be an advantage in an often shallow world. The important thing is not to give up on fellowshipping with others. When you're connected to a community, you're more empowered to uncover and live out the best, most purposeful version of yourself, mastering the second half of life with courage and compassion.

QUESTIONS

1. Do you tend to isolate or reach out to others when you are going through a difficult time? What are some reasons you might consider keeping to yourself?

2. What are some ways you need to catch up on the commandment to love others? In what ways can you close those gaps?

3. How can you make more of an effort to connect with and serve those in your church, community, and home?

4. How will you benefit once you connect more? How will it empower you to discover and pursue your purpose?

CHAPTER 5
THE PROBLEM WITH OPINIONS

Do you have fear of other people's opinions (FOPO) regarding God's purpose for your life?

How often do we compare our life situation to someone else's? Because we don't like where we are, we develop a fear of what others may think. We worry we're not where we ought to be financially, or maybe that we should've reached a certain status or position in our job by now (especially if we've been with the company for over ten years).

Some people are viewed negatively by family and friends due to reversals in their careers, marriages, or health. I often worried about what family members would have thought of me had my marriage ended in divorce. For better or for worse, the fear of a poor reputation frequently prevents people from ending their marriages when things are going south.

Beyond that, I worry about my wife and children's opinions. I'm concerned with whether they see me as a spiritual leader in our home. Oddly enough, my career transition into coaching and leadership development never caused concern for what others would think, perhaps because I never had to quit my job to follow my dream. Or, it could be because I knew in my heart that I was following God's purpose for my life. I was fundamentally motivated by the belief that one day, this experience might help someone else, rather than by concern for my reputation. I think having that approach helped to remove the "F" in FOPO.

Sharing my struggles with a trusted circle of friends brought me some relief. We often pray for each other and share our ups and downs. However, I sometimes experience pressure if one of my close friends seems to always have something good going on. As a brother, I'm excited for him, but a part of me may feel I need to "bring something to the conversation" for fear that others won't think my life is so hot.

I could allow my friends' successes to bring me so low that I stop coming around my circle. But comparing myself to others isn't only discouraging; it's sinful. Exodus 20:17 tells us, "You shall not covet your neighbor's house. You shall not covet your neighbor's wife, or his male or female servant, his ox or donkey, or anything that belongs to your neighbor." So, it's not God's will for us to desire another person's spouse, home, kids, or job. Instead, I've learned to view this tension as a vital source of accountability. Others will know if I'm slacking or failing to keep up with my responsibilities, so I've got to perform at my best.

Moreover, worrying about others' opinions is what the Bible calls a trap or snare. We learn, "Fear of man will prove to be a snare, but whoever trusts in the Lord is kept safe" (Proverbs 29:25). We're going to get ourselves into trouble if we're afraid of what other people think, but if we trust in God, we'll be kept safe.

OVERCOMING FOPO

Valuing the input of others is essential to your long-term success. For example, if you're considering starting a family or becoming a doctor, you'll want to talk to someone who's already taken that road. What potential problems can you expect? How can you start preparing now? Do you have the right personality makeup? Will you be happy with your economic and relational status in ten or twenty years of pursuing this goal?

The problem happens when we become so consumed with the opinions of others that we are unable to follow God's path for our lives. For example, you might feel God wants you to work in finance. Your talents, personality, and gifts align with this calling. However, your relatives believe that you should take over the family business. They will become angry and distant if you don't.

In this case, FOPO will limit your future. If you live to satisfy the opinions of others, you could end up pursuing the wrong goals and working in a field that doesn't fulfill you. In the long run, you could resent those who pushed you in the wrong direction, well-intentioned as they may have been.

Moreover, different people have different opinions about how we should conduct our lives. You may have relatives who think you should be a chef, a spouse who wants you to be an accountant, and professors who push you to teach. Eventually, you must accept the reality that you cannot make everyone happy. You need to choose a sensible path that aligns with God's will. Any road you choose will have trade-offs. Embrace the pros and cons and keep moving forward.

Living your life according to FOPO will lead to regular anxiety and unhappiness. There will always be people who don't like you; some may work with you or be in your extended family. If you're a people-pleaser, this can be a brutal reality to accept. However, you can be happy if you please the only One Whose opinions matter.

2 Timothy 1:7 says, "For the Spirit God gave us does not make us timid, but gives us power, love, and self-discipline." This is great news! God hasn't called you to be thin-skinned, getting buffeted in an ocean of worry and fear every time someone doesn't embrace you or approve of your choices. Instead, He has given you a powerful, disciplined Spirit. When we're walking in that Spirit, a little constructive criticism won't devastate us. Instead, we can incorpo-

rate the helpful parts of the feedback we receive into our daily practice. Moreover, competition won't overwhelm us. We can simply learn to do things better, achieving a different edge. We just need to focus on our Savior and see the work we have started through to completion.

No one else has your family, specific job, or unique responsibilities. God entrusted those to you because He believed you were capable. Worrying about the opinions of others will only distract you. Trusting God can help you keep your focus and find success without becoming conceited.

THE FEAR OF MOSES

Recall, if you will, the story of Moses. Moses led the nation of Israel out of slavery in Egypt into the Promised Land of Canaan after the twelve plagues finally convinced Pharaoh to let his free workforce go. Moses stretched out his hand and, with God's power, parted the Red Sea so God's people could walk across on dry land. In the morning, he extended it again so the water would refill the expanse and cover the entire Egyptian army. I assume I'm not telling you anything you don't already know.

What you may need to remember, however, is that Moses was not naturally a courageous guy. He was born during a time when Pharaoh was having all of the Hebrew baby boys in Egypt killed. The king feared the little nation would eventually take over the Egyptian kingdom. However, Moses was rescued when Pharaoh's daughter found him floating in the reeds, where his sister was hiding and watching him. The princess took him home and raised him as her own (Exodus 2:6-10).

Moses was raised with many Egyptian advantages in the house of Pharaoh, but he remained a Hebrew at heart. One day, he watched an Egyptian beating a Hebrew and became so angry that he killed the Egyptian man (Exodus 2:12). Afraid for his life, Moses fled to Midian, where he got married and had sons (Exodus 2:15-22). During

Moses' decades in the desert, the Pharaoh Moses knew died and was succeeded, and the Hebrew people cried out to God in their continued oppression (Exodus 2:23).

God had a vital calling for Moses' life, and his time finally came. God appeared to Moses in a burning bush, and Moses hid his face, afraid to look at Him (Exodus 3:1-6). God said,

> [10] "So now, go. I am sending you to Pharaoh to bring my people the Israelites out of Egypt."
>
> [11] But Moses said to God, "Who am I that I should go to Pharaoh and bring the Israelites out of Egypt?"
>
> [12] And God said, "I will be with you. And this will be the sign to you that it is I who have sent you: When you have brought the people out of Egypt, you will worship God on this mountain."
>
> [13] Moses said to God, "Suppose I go to the Israelites and say to them, 'The God of your fathers has sent me to you,' and they ask me, 'What is his name?' Then what shall I tell them?"
>
> [14] God said to Moses, "I am who I am. This is what you are to say to the Israelites: 'I am has sent me to you.'" (Exodus 3:10-14)

Notice what Moses didn't say. He didn't cry out, "Yes, Lord! What a terrible thing this Pharaoh is doing! I can't wait to turn him into Egyptian fava beans!"

Instead, Moses said, "Why are you calling me? I'm not qualified for this role" (verse 11).

And God's response was simply, "I will be with you" (verse 12). He didn't say, "C'mon Moses, you'll be a great leader. You've got all the right education and snazzy leather sandals for it." God promised only His presence, because that was going to be enough.

Moses was hiding in the desert out of fear, not courage. He was angry about the oppression His people were suffering, but he wasn't eager to rescue anybody.

And Moses' concern didn't stop there. He was afraid that the Hebrews wouldn't believe God had sent him. So, the Lord provided two miracles that Moses could use to prove His hand in the mission (Exodus 4:1-9). Yet Moses wasn't done worrying.

[10] Moses said to the Lord, "Pardon your servant, Lord. I have never been eloquent, neither in the past nor since you have spoken to your servant. I am slow of speech and tongue."

[11] The Lord said to him, "Who gave human beings their mouths? Who makes them deaf or mute? Who gives them sight or makes them blind? Is it not I, the Lord? [12] Now go; I will help you speak and will teach you what to say."

[13] But Moses said, "Pardon your servant, Lord. Please send someone else."

[14] Then the Lord's anger burned against Moses and he said, "What about your brother, Aaron the Levite? I know he can speak well. He is already on his way to meet you, and he will be glad to see you. [15] You shall speak to him and put words in his mouth; I will help both of you speak and will teach you what to do. [16] He will speak to the people for you, and it will be as if he were your mouth and as if you were God to him. [17] But take this staff in your hand so you can perform the signs with it." (Exodus 4:10-17)

Moses told God he had never been much of an orator. In response, God reminded him Who gave him his mouth in the first place. Finally, Moses told God to choose another man. This made God angry, but He suggested that Moses enlist the help of his more verbally inclined brother. He also said that He would continue showing He was with Moses through signs.

Isn't that how some of us often view God's calling? We think it's too lofty for us and remind God we aren't worthy. We bring up our shortcomings and sometimes ask Him to choose a different person. Yet God says that all that matters is that He will be with us. Moses assumed he could not carry out his assignment because of his shortcomings and physical challenges. God, however, was not worried.

It's also important to note that, in the end, Moses obeyed God, despite all of his hesitations and insecurities. Our upbringings and experiences may have given us what we feel are pretty good reasons to be afraid, but He calls us to do as He says anyway. Don't let fear become an excuse to avoid doing what you know you need to do.

When God has given you a purpose, He will not fail. Other people will have their opinions and doubts about you, but you can do all things through the One Who gives us strength (Philippians 4:13). The next time you are tempted to take criticism or ridicule to heart, look up. God says you are enough, and He is all you need for the mission.

QUESTIONS

1. What decisions have you made based on the opinions of others? Would you have made different choices if you weren't worried about what they thought?
2. What part of Moses' story can you relate to? Have you ever believed you were unworthy of God's call on your life? What do you think God thinks about your limits?
3. How could minimizing the role of others' opinions in your life help you to accomplish more?

CHAPTER 6
SELF WORTH VS. GOD-WORTH

As we continue to discuss God's purpose for our lives, it is crucial to add an important foundation: the difference between self-worth and God-worth. The world clamors for self-worth, and most of us spend our lives trying to earn it. Pursuing self-worth can even hinder us from finding and fulfilling our true purpose. But pursuing our true purpose leads to something greater and more substantial than a fleeting sense of self-worth: God-worth. Understanding our purpose and understanding our worth in Who God is and what He's done for us go hand in hand. This chapter will flesh out this important idea.

As an introverted kid growing up in Memphis, Tennessee, I wanted to be accepted by others. I know most of you can relate! Specifically, I grew up in Parkway Village in Southeast Memphis, where you had to learn how to "check." These were quick-witted, humorous jokes or insults based on someone's physical appearance or other traits. Checking is also commonly referred to as "playing the dozens." You could quickly become popular if you could "check" someone and make others laugh. Unbeknownst to me at the time, "playing the dozens" originated in the 18th-century New Orleans slave trade, where enslaved Africans who were either deformed at birth or mutilated as a result of disobedience were sold in dozens at a cheaper price.

The need for social acceptance continued through junior high school, especially since I was the new kid. I felt I needed to hang out with the popular kids to gain some identity. On top of that, teenage hormones kicked in, and I began to crave attention from girls. The attention I received boosted my fragile self-confidence and in turn further fueled my need for social acceptance. Earlier in my childhood, I was shy and self-conscious about my appearance—particularly my dark skin. In the late 1980s, light or fair-skinned men were considered by society to be more physically attractive, as evidenced by the number of light-skinned celebrities, actors, and models who gained popularity in that decade. Few dark-skinned men were considered sex symbols until the early 1990s, when men like Michael Jordan made the dark-skinned, bald look famous. Therefore, when I was in school, I was an easy target for ridicule when it came to checking, and for several years of my youth, I actually hated being dark-skinned.

Society's standards for attractiveness are constantly changing. All it takes is one celebrity to popularize a particular body type or style of dress. Folks in the 1960s would never have thought that wearing your pajamas to the grocery store would be expected, or that dressing up in public could make you seem pretentious. Those living in the skinny-obsessed 1990s couldn't have imagined a time when fuller body types were a beauty standard. Yet God doesn't make mistakes. Our personalities' physical and emotional attributes are precisely as He wants them to be.

As a young man, I never really took the time to think about my identity. I learned about God and verses in His Word that pertained to how He viewed me, but I never really took them to heart. I guess because of the way I was living, I never felt worthy to be regarded the way God views me. I don't think I was a bad person, but I had committed enough sin to feel unworthy. Even today, I struggle with bouts of feeling undeserving of His love.

Though I was taught that I am the righteousness of God through Christ Jesus early in my life, that truth's relationship to my true identity never sank in. If I'm honest, I used it to excuse sinful behavior throughout my life. Yes, God loves me, and because I am in Christ, my sins are forgiven, past, present, and future—and I will go to heaven when I die. But that's not something to take for granted. His Grace is NOT a free pass to continue willfully and intentionally living a life of sin. I wrestled with genuinely embracing and living by this concept for years. Part of the difficulty was that I allowed the way I viewed myself, my style, and my talk to be shaped by my environment. To be accepted by my culture's standards, I let these norms define my identity. Still, God continued to love me and draw me to Himself. By His grace, I am finally beginning to see myself the way He does.

SECURITY IN GOD

Unlike the world's unreliable standards of worth, the security God offers cannot be undone by anyone. Look again at Romans 8:38-39, which tells us,

> [38] For I am convinced that neither death nor life, neither angels nor demons, neither the present nor the future, nor any powers, [39] neither height nor depth nor anything else in all creation, will be able to separate us from the love of God that is in Christ Jesus our Lord.

God is still with you when you sin, fail, or get lost on your way to Jersey. The truth is that all of our worries and anxiety fall away once we turn to our Savior. In Matthew 6:31-34, He said,

[31] "So do not worry, saying, 'What shall we eat?' or 'What shall we drink?' or 'What shall we wear?' [32] For the pagans run after all these things, and your heavenly Father knows that you need them. [33] But seek first his kingdom and his righteousness, and all these things will be given to you as well. [34] Therefore do not worry about tomorrow, for tomorrow will worry about itself. Each day has enough trouble of its own."

Jesus said that unbelievers worry about what they're going to eat. We are called not to worry about what will happen tomorrow, because He is already there, and He's taking care of things. If you are a believer, it's contradictory to operate from a place of anxiety.

God doesn't give us a Spirit of fear but one of "power, love and self-discipline" (2 Timothy 1:7). Think about the concerns that keep you from living authentically and with purpose. Is there someone you're comparing yourself to who makes you feel you can't measure up? How can you begin to take on a new perspective, an outlook that will allow you to live more authentically in God?

I know that this begins in my heart when I finally accept that God loves me, no matter what. I must remind myself of this daily, until it deepens my spirit. There will be moments when I feel unworthy of His love and tender mercy. During these times, I can hold that thought against His Word and reject it, because it's contrary to the truth. Romans 8:1 says, "Therefore, there is now no condemnation for those who are in Christ Jesus."

The apostle Paul told us to "take captive every thought to make it obedient to Christ" (2 Corinthians 10:5b). You can't let thoughts run around your head or control your mindset if they go against the Word of God. This includes our worries, doubts, and insecurities. Unlike our sins, which can be challenging to part with, letting go of your negative thinking will provide immediate relief! Don't allow your concerns to weigh you down. Instead, remind yourself of how secure you are in your Savior's love.

GOD'S PROMISES

In Isaiah 54:1-5, Israel was addressed as a barren woman because her numbers had decreased. Still, she was encouraged to sing in anticipation of the increase that was about to happen:

> [1] "Sing, barren woman,
>   you who never bore a child;
> burst into song, shout for joy,
>   you who were never in labor;
> because more are the children of the desolate
>   woman
>   than of her who has a husband,"
> says the Lord.
> [2] "Enlarge the place of your tent,
>   stretch your tent curtains wide,
>   do not hold back;
> lengthen your cords,
>   strengthen your stakes.
> [3] For you will spread out to the right and to the left;
>   your descendants will dispossess nations
>   and settle in their desolate cities.
> [4] "Do not be afraid; you will not be put to shame.
>   Do not fear disgrace; you will not be humiliated.
> You will forget the shame of your youth
>   and remember no more the reproach of your
>   widowhood.
> [5] For your Maker is your husband—
>   the Lord Almighty is his name—
> the Holy One of Israel is your Redeemer;
>   He is called the God of all the earth."

In verse 2, God told Israel to increase her tents, or dwelling places, to get ready for the increase she could expect. In verse 3, He talked about expansions, saying that the tiny seed of Israel would inherit the Gentiles.

Israel was experiencing a time of great disappointment and loss, but God still had a plan for her! She would increase beyond her expectations. So it is with us in our desert seasons. God does not want us to seek meaning and comfort in people, drugs, or food. He wants us to lean on Him, because He has a plan, and He will see it through.

Verse 8 of the same chapter says, "'In a surge of anger I hid my face from you for a moment, but with everlasting kindness I will have compassion on you,' says the Lord your Redeemer." In other words, God becomes angry when we disobey Him, but that wrath will not endure. Instead, His kindness and compassion take precedence. God's grace knows no bounds.

In verses 16 and 17, we learn that even the negative things that happen to us are under our Father's control:

> [16] "See, it is I who created the blacksmith
> who fans the coals into flame
> and forges a weapon fit for its work.
> And it is I who have created the destroyer to wreak
>   havoc;
> [17] no weapon forged against you will prevail,
> and you will refute every tongue that accuses you.
> This is the heritage of the servants of the Lord,
> and this is their vindication from me,"
>   declares the Lord. (Isaiah 54:16-17)

God created the very blacksmith who forged the weapons people use against us, and He says they will not prevail. We will one day refute every tongue that accuses us. No one will be able to injure you with their accusations. If others charge you with imposture and deceit, you will be able to convince them of their error. By manifestation of the truth, you will condemn them.

Our enemies may, for a time, be permitted to appear to prosper. Yet theirs will be a partial success. The Lord will vindicate us. When you're looking for absolute security, the only place to look is up. Everything else only provides a temporary escape.

THE GOOD SHEPHERD

Whenever I'm tempted to look for security in things other than Jesus, I remind myself of John 10:11-18, where He said,

11 "I am the good shepherd. The good shepherd lays down his life for the sheep. 12 The hired hand is not the shepherd and does not own the sheep. So when he sees the wolf coming, he abandons the sheep and runs away. Then the wolf attacks the flock and scatters it. 13 The man runs away because he is a hired hand and cares nothing for the sheep.

14 "I am the good shepherd; I know my sheep and my sheep know me— 15 just as the Father knows me and I know the Father— and I lay down my life for the sheep. 16 I have other sheep that are not of this sheep pen. I must bring them also. They too will listen to my voice, and there shall be one flock and one shepherd. 17 The reason my Father loves me is that I lay down my life—only to take it up again. 18 No one takes it from me, but I lay it down of my own accord. I have authority to lay it down and authority to take it up again. This command I received from my Father."

While we sheep are grazing aimlessly around for grass, we don't see the wolf approaching. Our false idols, such as our material possessions, romantic partners, or pornography, will not alert us to danger. They are the hired hands who pretend to care, but won't stand up for us when things are difficult. They will let our own devices gobble us up.

This is not the case with Jesus. He will always stand up for us, even to the point of laying down His life. We live in an insecure world, and things we hadn't planned will always occur. When those times come, we need a Shepherd Who will not abandon us. We need Someone Who will do whatever it takes to save us, even at a significant cost to Himself. We need to understand our God-worth.

The next time you're tempted to run to friends, money, or fantasies when things go wrong, think again. Jesus will not reject you, and you can always trust His leadership.

QUESTIONS:

1. Were you ever teased or made fun of as a child? How have those thoughts and impressions remained with you to this day?
2. What are some reasons you might sometimes feel unworthy of God's love?
3. How can you begin to take your thoughts of unworthiness captive and replace them with security in God's love?
4. What is the relationship between knowing our God-worth and pursuing His purpose for our lives?

CHAPTER 7
PURPOSE IN MARRIAGE

My wife and I met in 2002 at a sorority party. We had seen each other on campus and even took a class together (though we didn't interact often in class, as I could barely stay awake!). One of my fraternity brothers introduced us, and her attractiveness captivated me. A few months later, I ran into her at a local nightclub and found the courage to ask if she had a boyfriend. When she told me she didn't, I asked for her number.

We dated off and on for about a year and became an exclusive couple around Christmas of 2003. The following November, I landed a new job and planned a small family dinner at a local Italian restaurant. I proposed, and she accepted. Today, we have four children: Tyler, Morgan, Daniel, and Penelope.

Over the last eighteen years, we have had our share of ups and downs. As with all marriages, family trips, holidays, and Christmas mornings were peak experiences. However, pornography and flirtation crept in, and our union hit a severe rough patch in 2017. I had a two-year affair with a coworker that had started as an innocent conversation. We became pretty attached, and I failed to support my wife because the emotional part of myself was tied up elsewhere.

Marriage is a topic that may not seem immediately connected to the discovery of your purpose in life. It may seem like God's greater design for you and the way in which you communicate with your spouse are two separate, albeit important, things. But you won't become the kind of person who can walk faithfully in the purpose God is calling you to if you don't start by walking faithfully in the marriage He called you to. Our spouses will be our greatest supporters and our most enthusiastic cheerleaders, but not if we aren't there for them in the same way. I know my marriage isn't the only one that has had to overcome mistrust after unfaithfulness, but even if that's not your situation, the lessons I've learned can help you find wholeness in your relationship, providing a solid foundation for you to grow into what God has planned for you.

God's Word talks about being unable to serve two masters (Matthew 6:24). While this verse discusses the conflict between God and money ("you will hate the one and love the other"), you can easily apply it to extramarital affairs. You cannot be wholly devoted to two different romantic partners at once.

God hates divorce. When you marry, it's understood that both partners will continue to do the hard work, even when feelings don't carry the day. This perfects the work of love that He began. Our marriage now has to struggle against mistrust, hurt, and insecurity. If I had made better decisions, that wouldn't be the case.

Many days, it feels like our relationship is moving "two steps forward, three steps back." I can sense when my wife is putting walls up. Recently, I shared with her the joyful news that we were putting a bonus room onto the house and that work would begin soon. She wasn't excited about it the way I hoped she would be. Instead, she was upset that I hadn't discussed the change with her beforehand.

You can learn lessons from all your mistakes. In my case, the need to be transparent and communicate before making big decisions became apparent. I know that in many marriages, people become more like roommates with children than a mature husband-and-wife team. For us to be the latter, I need to take responsibility for this shortcoming, without beating myself up. I also need to communicate more often and more effectively going forward.

One thing I am grateful for is that, as we discussed in the last chapter, there is now no shame or condemnation for those in Christ Jesus (Romans 8:1). Despite my failures, God still has a purpose for my life, and I intend to fulfill it. God's plan for our lives will prevail, no matter what. Proverbs 19:21 says, "Many are the plans in a person's heart, but it is the Lord's purpose that prevails." We have many ideas about how our lives should go, but God's plan is the one that will win out in the end. Still, it remains up to us to discover our skills and gifts, learning how to use them for His glory.

FORGIVENESS IN MARRIAGE

Many marriages overcome infidelity and other hurdles. As I discovered, the first step is owning up to our mistakes. This doesn't mean excusing them or saying things like "It was a difficult time" or "You weren't there for me." You've got to admit to your part in hurting the other person, whether your actions were justified or not.

Marriage is a beautiful place to learn the art of patience. When you ask for forgiveness, you may need to wait for the other person to process emotions and develop trust again before they can grant it. Telling your spouse that they are overreacting or dismissing their feelings will lead to greater distance.

There will also be times when you must forgive your partner for things that hurt you. While forgiveness can be painful, you must consciously decide that you will refuse to wallow in bitterness, no matter what happened in the past. Instead, you will forgive your spouse, since Jesus has forgiven you so much (Matthew 6:14).

Forgiveness is for the forgiver's benefit as well as the forgiven. You will be healthier, both physically and mentally. You'll enjoy better self-esteem, lower blood pressure, and a more robust immune system. By contrast, holding a grudge can lead to depression, irritability, and anxiousness.[1] Forgiveness will also set a strong example for your children. It's essential, however, to remember that forgiving someone doesn't necessarily mean trusting. Many spouses resist forgiveness because they aren't ready to trust their partners again after trust was broken.

Rebuilding trust in a relationship requires plenty of time. You'll need to be willing to forgo dwelling on the past and focus on honest communication. Open up to each other about how you've been hurt and what you need from your partner. These conversations are often tough to have, but they can bring you closer together and make you more compassionate.

When you're talking to your partner, avoid accusing or criticizing them, as this will only make them feel more ashamed and alone. Instead, show lots of empathy and even humor (when appropriate) when having heart-to-heart talks. This will go a long way toward showing your partner that you are on their side.

We are often drawn to other people because we lack a sense of acceptance at home. If you look forward to seeing your coworker a little too much, step back and ask yourself, "What is this person giving me that I like? Can I work on developing this with my spouse?"

Many couples find it helps to talk to a marriage counselor when they begin experiencing problems. If you're willing to change, your marriage can become a partnership between two mature adults. None of us marry the perfect spouse, but we can become people others admire if we will honestly take account of our strengths, our flaws, and the person God wants us to be.

---

1. "Forgiveness: Letting Go of Grudges and Bitterness," Mayo Clinic, November 22, 2022, https://www.mayoclinic.org/healthy-lifestyle/adult-health/in-depth/forgive ness/art-20047692.

FORGIVING YOURSELF

People sometimes get stuck in sin because they find it difficult to forgive themselves. We aren't internalizing God's forgiveness, so we may continue to beat ourselves up or try to make up for our sins and mistakes through human effort, which is a surefire way to fall down the sin rabbit hole again. We will turn back to old habits in order to assuage the pain and insecurity that arise when we inevitably fail.

2 Corinthians 5:17-18 tells us, "Therefore, if anyone is in Christ, the new creation has come: The old has gone, the new is here! All this is from God, who reconciled us to himself through Christ and gave us the ministry of reconciliation." We are new creatures because we have accepted Christ as our Lord and Savior. This means that we had a *different* identity before Christ's coming, death, and resurrection. We were sinful beings, without any human perfection to commend us, because the Bible tells us everyone has sinned and can't live up to God's glory (Romans 3:23).

Yet, once we have accepted Christ, everything associated with that old identity gets washed away. The old has gone, and the new has come! This new creation thinks and behaves differently. It has taken on the mindset, likeness, and image of the Creator. We are now a reflection of the King and considered Kingdom citizens.

So how do we keep ourselves from falling back into an old mindset of sin and low self-esteem?

Well, it starts with renewing our minds daily with God's Word. Romans 12:2 tells us, "Do not conform to the pattern of this world, but be transformed by the renewing of your mind. Then you will be able to test and approve what God's will is—his good, pleasing and perfect will."

Are you making time daily to read the Word and remind yourself of your new identity in Christ? Are you meditating on Scriptures, such as, "in all these things we are more than conquerors through him who loved us" (Romans 8:37)?

When you feel lost, you'll never find strength, renewal, and a solid identity in another person, a job, or the internet. You will only find it in your Savior. Don't be afraid to dig into the Word when you need peace of mind. Frequently, God is the only One Who can provide it.

2 Corinthians 5:18 ("All this is from God, who reconciled us to himself through Christ and gave us the ministry of reconciliation") implies that God has given us a mission, or a purpose. We are here to help reconcile the world back to Him. We are charged with sharing the Good News of Christ and His love with others. You are still on earth because God has an essential job for you to do. You must reach those in your family, ministry, or workplace for Christ. You are no longer an ordinary sinner, wandering through life, seeking temporary peace. Jesus gives you the forgiveness, love, and power you need to reach the world for Him.

Still, you've got to be in a good spiritual place yourself to set a strong example. Don't criticize yourself about your mistakes when your mind drifts toward sin. You'll need to take responsibility, because failing to do so will only lead to more significant spiritual issues. But you also need to be able to accept Christ's forgiveness and move on. He already knew all about your sin before He called you— and yet, He still called you.

2 Corinthians 7:10 says, "Godly sorrow brings repentance that leads to salvation and leaves no regret, but worldly sorrow brings death." When you mess up, allow yourself to feel sorry for your mistake and turn back to your Savior, but refuse to loll around in shame. Guilt is appropriate only when it leads you to change your ways and move on, continuing to fulfill the mission God placed on your life.

If you are someone who tends to criticize yourself when you sin, learn to catch the negative voices as soon as they start pointing fingers at you. If you have experienced past abuse, this may be more difficult and could require the help of a licensed therapist. Refuse to drown in the lake of negative messages. Instead, lift yourself daily with Scriptures that remind you of your identity in Him. Put them in your wallet or dashboard if you have to, but always be saturating your mind with Scripture.

THE FORGIVEN SINNER IN MARRIAGE

Forgiveness will benefit your physical health as well as your relationships. A compassionate attitude toward yourself and your spouse makes it easier to admit and move on from your mistakes. You won't constantly hide your sins from one another, because you won't be afraid of your partner's reaction.

Ruth Graham once said, "A happy marriage is the union of two good forgivers." Graham is best known as the wife of famed evangelist Billy Graham. Interestingly, her point is that in marriage, sin and hurt are inevitable, as they are in every other part of life. You may even do something to help your spouse that could inadvertently cause pain.

It's important not to write your husband or wife off when they make mistakes, thinking you deserve a daily fairy tale. Instead, you must remember your own flaws and quickly extend forgiveness to the other. Eventually, you could be that happy older couple, holding hands on your rocking chairs as you enter your sunset years.

HOLISTIC PURPOSE

I want to end the chapter by saying that to pursue your personal purpose without a more holistic consideration of your life will leave you fragmented. I included this chapter on marital forgiveness because my own sense of purpose would be pointless if my wife and I had not committed to a good marriage of forgiveness. Betrayal is a serious issue that is difficult to overcome, but not only can Jesus help you overcome it, He can even fold the experience into your overall life purpose. In fact, including this chapter in the book is allowing me to partially fulfill my purpose in life of helping others. By God's grace, I want to be transparent about my failures so that others can see the power of God in my life.

QUESTIONS

1. What are some good reasons people get married? What are some foolish reasons?
2. If you're married, what mistakes have you made in your marriage that you may be tempted to replay in your mind? How can you get off that roller coaster?
3. What are some ways you can be more forgiving toward yourself? How will that impact your pursuit of your purpose in life?
4. How can you be more forgiving toward your spouse (or others in your life), allowing them to open up to you?

CHAPTER 8

KNOW YOUR PERSONALITY AND TALENTS

H ere's a question for you. Have you ever stopped to think about what makes you *you*? We've all at one time or another had a conversation about someone's personality in which you or the other person said, "Well, that's just the way they are." Or maybe you were the topic of the conversation, and you admitted, "That's just the way I am." I can recall when my oldest son, Tyler, tried out for tee ball at seven years old. At his first practice, the coach raved about his ability to hit the ball and his incredible speed. He would always say to us, "Tyler's a natural!" And even though he didn't stick with tee ball for long (eventually finding his passion for football), we knew that Tyler possessed natural athletic talents. So what exactly is that thing that shapes *your* personality? Moreover, what talents do you have that no one knows about?

Dr. Elmer Towns, an author, lecturer, and seminary professor, described personality as a matter of the heart. An individual's intellect, perception, reasoning, and emotions are all housed there. God used so many biblical characters despite their personality flaws. I often liken myself to David, a man God described as someone "after

[His] own heart" (Acts 13:22). I identify with his humility and desire to worship God, despite his mistakes.

Purpose is wrapped up in helping others, and it must suit our unique personality and giftings. Let's examine those.

IMPORTANT PERSONALITY TRAITS

When I was a teen in the 90s, it was common to describe someone else's personality as either "good" or "bad." You might not be attracted to someone because they had a "bad" personality, but you probably wouldn't have been able to provide many specifics as to what made it unappealing to you.

The truth is that there are no "bad" personality types, just different ones. One problem with today's career world is that many people are square pegs in round holes, looking to succeed in professions and industries they aren't naturally suited for. Tools like the Myers-Briggs personality test are helpful here.

Isabel Briggs Myers and her mother, Katherine Cook Briggs, introduced the formal personality test in 1943. At the end of World War II, the Office of Strategic Services (a predecessor to the CIA) used it to help suitably assign intelligence operatives in Europe. It was soon widely used to help guide young people into the right professions.[1] Today, corporations often adopt it to help build morale and awareness of individuals' different strengths and weaknesses.

The four preference pairs in Myers Briggs highlight different aspects of people's personalities. These pairs are Extrovert (E) or Introvert (I), Sensing (S) or Intuition (I), Thinking (T) or Feeling (F), and Judging (J) or Perceiving (P). A person's combination of their natural tendencies in each of these pairs is their particular personality type.[2]

1. Melissa Block, "How the Myers-Briggs Personality Test Began in a Mother's Living Room Lab," NPR, September 22, 2018, https://www.npr.org/2018/09/22/650019038/how-the-myers-briggs-personality-test-began-in-a-mothers-living-room-lab.
2. "The 16 MBTI® Personality Types," Myers and Briggs Foundation, accessed

The first pair, Extrovert vs. Introvert, deals with how you interact with the world around you. Extroverts love to engage with others and get energized by social interactions. These folks are natural teachers, managers, HR professionals, and salespeople. In churches, they excel as Bible study leaders, Sunday school teachers, and youth ministers. If you can't get enough of your social time, and if spending time with others fills you with delight and curiosity, you should look into ventures suited to Extroverts.

Conversely, Introverts are quiet and thoughtful. While they enjoy social interaction, they tend to prefer calmer environments. Introverts can find socializing tiring. They are usually energized by time alone or with someone they're close to, taking in nature or enjoying a deep conversation. Introverts might find it most fulfilling to work in an independent job like accounting, writing, or designing. Introverts might be comfortable creating bulletins, VBS sets, or websites for their church. They might also like more front-facing activities like singing or teaching, but they may prefer to do these things in a smaller setting or in a role where they can blend in, such as working with a small teen Bible study or playing bass guitar with the church band.

You may be reading this and thinking, "Wow, I think I might be an Extrovert *and* an Introvert. I identify with the qualities of both." While most of us have a mix of extroverted and introverted qualities, true ambiverts are an intriguing hybrid. They require social interaction *and* alone time, finding both exhausting if they don't regularly switch between them. These folks may enjoy work that requires elements of both socialization and solitude, such as teaching or web designing.[3]

The second personality contrast pair in the Myers-Briggs system

---

August 5, 2024, https://www.myersbriggs.org/my-mbti-personality-type/the-16-mbti-personality-types/.

3. Sarah Regan, "7 Signs You May Be An Ambivert & How To Thrive, From Personality Experts," mindbodygreen, June 30, 2022, https://www.mindbodygreen.com/articles/ambivert-meaning-and-signs#:

is Sensing (S) vs. Intuition (I). Those who dominate in Sensing tend to thrive on data they can observe with their five senses. What does a situation look, feel, or smell like? Sensors will draw their conclusions based on these details. You may find them describing experiences with clear, comprehensive terms that give you an accurate picture. Doctors, psychologists, and artists are just some examples of professions that would suit someone with a strength for sensing.

The contrast for this is people who think intuitively. That means they are eager to explore the possibilities that the sensory data suggests. They aren't interested only in what they can see or touch. These people have active imaginations and enjoy working as financial advisors, architects, or entrepreneurs. They love to use their creativity in concert with concrete facts.

Between Thinkers (T) and Feelers (F), Thinkers emphasize facts and statistical information more. These individuals make decisions based on logic rather than feelings. Thinkers are great with data, engineering, and chemical sciences. They are also wonderful people to talk about decisions with you when you are at a crossroads. A Thinker won't allow you to let your feelings make a decision that wouldn't make any logical sense or bring you long-term happiness.

Those who are Feelers (F) will always involve emotions in conclusions. These people are good at considering the feelings of others, and they might be gifted writers, artists, and therapists. The key to success is for Feelers to know when to allow feelings to guide them and when to deprioritize emotions in favor of a more logical thought process.

Finally, the fourth scale involves Judgers (J) versus Perceivers (P). Judging people enjoy having a clearly marked path. Judgers like well-defined standards and rules so they know precisely what is expected of them to be successful. Lawyers, school administrators, and doctors benefit from a Judging personality bent.

Perceivers, however, are more flexible. They will handle problems as they develop and spend as much time on a task as they feel it requires. These individuals tend to be warm, caring, and curious.

They know things sometimes aren't black and white and seek to understand before they conclude. Perceivers excel at work with children or as craftsmen.

Your combination of four main types will make up your Myers-Briggs personality type, which can give you an accurate idea of the kind of work that will be the most comfortable and satisfying for you. For example, someone whose personality type is Introvert/Intuitive/Thinking/Perceiving (INTP) may be constantly thinking, making them well-suited to be authors or business analysts. It may also cause them to be too cerebral if they aren't careful, which means they may want to surround themselves with family and friends who help them laugh and see the lighter side of life.

Your role in your profession or church should take your personality type into consideration. If you're an Introvert (I), you may be attracted to church leadership but realize that speaking publicly may not be your strong suit. You can find ways to lead in a context that may be more comfortable for you, such as serving on the board or in the church office. If you're a Judger (J), you may be involved in creating a church handbook or a list of rules for the children's ministry that everyone will agree on and find easy to follow. Those who are Feelers (F) may wish to work hands-on with individuals who are hurting.

Myers-Briggs and other personality tests, such as DISC and the Clifton Strengths Assessment (formerly Strengths Finder), can help you determine the best role for your internal makeup. DISC defines personality in four major categories:

- Dominance: active use of force to overcome resistance in the environment
- Inducement: use of charm in order to deal with obstacles
- Submission: warm and voluntary acceptance of the need to fulfill a request

- Compliance: fearful adjustment to a superior force.[4]

The Clifton Strengths Assessment will measure your personality based on your natural patterns of feeling and thinking, rating you in 34 strength categories. These assessments aren't free, but figuring out more of your makeup may be worth the time and money. When you know your strengths, you won't struggle trying to shine where it's difficult for you. You can also talk to your church leaders about how you can be evaluated to find the best role in your congregation.

The Body of Christ with many parts that Paul talks about in 1 Corinthians 12:12-27 acknowledges that our congregations comprise many different types of people. We can't tell each other, "I don't need you," just because we don't all function similarly (verses 21-22). Instead, we must learn to appreciate the disparate strengths of others and how they can complement our own. "If they were all one part, where would the body be? As it is, there are many parts, but one body" (verses 19-20).

KNOW YOUR TALENTS

Hand-in-hand with your personality are your talents. The dictionary calls a talent "a special, often athletic, creative, or artistic aptitude," or "general intelligence or mental power."[5]

Talents are more concrete than personality types, and many of you already knew what your abilities were when you were young. Perhaps you could write, paint, or cut wood better than anyone else. Maybe you had a sweet jump shot or could run a faster mile than your friends.

I discovered my love of drawing when I was only ten years old. I created fictional characters (rap artists) who mimicked the music I

---

4. "Disc Assessment," Wikipedia, July 25, 2024, https://en.wikipedia.org/wiki/DISC_assessment.

5. *Merriam-Webster Dictionary*, s.v. "talent (*n.*)," accessed April 1, 2024, https://www.merriam-webster.com/dictionary/talent.

listened to. Eventually, I was developing comic book characters with stories inspired by movies. I didn't realize that God had placed these gifts in me, only that I loved to draw.

Some people are great with critical thinking, organizing, or design. You may also have natural people skills, such as listening, persuading, and peacemaking. Some talents manifest immediately, while others need to be fine-tuned over time.

Make a list of all the things you did well as a kid. Are you still talented in those areas? Are there ways you can use them to reach the lost, such as mentoring foster kids through one-on-one basketball? Could you design sets for your church? How about at work? Could your excellent storytelling skills be used to build your company?

If you aren't sure of your talents, look at how you spend your leisure time. Are you usually doodling, humming, or reading? You may be drawn to those activities because you have a degree of success with them. Reach out to family and friends for advice. They may say something like, "I notice that your nieces and nephews love you. Have you ever considered working with children?" You may not even recognize an aptitude as a talent because it comes so easily to you. Others, on the other hand, may see what you do well and envy your skill.

Many talent aptitude tests exist as well. If you're interested in taking one, a great place to start is your HR department or church ministry director. You may discover you are gifted in many ways and can be a blessing in many lives. The Bible says, "Each of you should use whatever gift you have received to serve others, as faithful stewards of God's grace in its various forms" (1 Peter 4:10). We are commanded to be good stewards of what He has given us and reminded not to waste our talents.

Proverbs 18:16 says, "A gift opens the way and ushers the giver into the presence of the great." We must study our craft and strengthen our skills so that we show ourselves approved (2 Timothy 2:15).

Our purpose comes at the intersection of our gifts and the challenges we overcome. Sometimes, you may feel like no one understands you and everything is your fault. While you may bear some responsibility for your circumstances, you should not give up. God will not allow you to face your challenges alone. The Holy Spirit is with those of us who are believers. He listens and wants to talk to us every day. We were created to commune with God and fellowship with Him through prayer and meditation.

Quietly reflect on what God's Word may tell you about your situation. Believe that whatever you're going through is ultimately for your good.

God does not want you to reach the middle of your life and regretfully look behind you. Instead, He wants you to look forward to how you can use your experience, gifts, and life lessons to build others up. He has an essential purpose for you that can begin right now.

QUESTIONS:

1. Before taking the Myers-Briggs test, where do you think your personality will fall between the different pairs (Introversion/Extroversion, Sensing/Intuition, Thinking/Feeling, and Judging/Perceiving)? What aspects of your personality are you unsure of?
2. Are there any ministries or professional roles you haven't considered but might want to learn more about?
3. What natural talents do you have that others could benefit from, and how could you get started using them?

CHAPTER 9
THE IMPORTANCE OF VISION

If you've ever tried to start a new business or ministry, you know the importance of vision. Your audience gets complicated, people quit, and problems to solve suddenly consume your time. The balloon carrying you above the fray is your dream, also known as your vision. Your vision reminds you that one day, all of your striving will be worth it, allowing you to see success in a brand-new way. No one said it would be easy, but you're prepared to endure the bad weather if it means you'll tangibly see what before you could only imagine.

The Bible says, "Where there is no vision, the people perish: but he that keepeth the law, happy is he" (Proverbs 29:18 KJV). The Book of Wisdom says that people will suffer when they can't see the big picture, yet those who follow God's Word will be happy. Your vision must align with your heavenly Father's commands to be fulfilled. Then, you will be blessed, even during difficult times.

The dictionary defines *vision* as "the act and power of seeing" and "a thought, concept, or object formed by the imagination."[1] When you have a vision, you possess a plan for the future. The late Dr. Myles Munroe shared the following excerpt from one of his many teachings on self-discipline:

> Vision is supposed to be the source of your human motivation. It simplifies your life...Most people are poor because no one knows who they are. Vision helps you identify yourself before the people in the world. And because they know who you are, they know what to come to you for...Become so good in an area that they can't ignore you.[2]

And in another sermon, he further said: "If you want to be successful in life, do not seek success. Seek to become a person of value."[3]

In other words, just as I asked at the beginning of chapter eight: What gifts and talents make you *you*? Finding the answer to this question could be the very thing to help us rediscover who we are and the purpose that God has for our lives. If we reflect on this for a moment, we realize that vision is vital for our lives. It helps us to declare the type of life that we desire to live. It gives us something to aspire to, pursue, and work towards. It gives us something bigger than ourselves as our legacy, which we pass along from generation to generation. And because vision gives us something to pursue, there is a direct correlation between having vision and living out our purpose.

According to Dr. Munroe, vision helps to clarify our purpose. So, if we want to rediscover our identity and purpose, we must regain a

1. *Merriam-Webster Dictionary*, s.v. "vision (n.)," accessed March 27, 2024, https://www.merriam-webster.com/dictionary/vision.
2. Myles Munroe, "Chasing Your Dream by Dr. Myles Munroe," Pneuma Tv, March 28, 2019, Youtube video, 1:35 to 2:30, https://www.youtube.com/watch?v=Ye1NJBZroVk.
3. Myles Munroe, "The 5 Kingdom Keys For Business Success | Dr. Myles Munroe," Munroe Global, May 2, 2021, Youtube video, 1:01:16 to 1:01:41, https://www.youtube.com/watch?v=muZ3_2esQuQ.

clear life vision. The gifts and talents that God has placed in each of us make us all unique, and I believe they were given to us to foster vision for our lives. If we can each take personal inventory and tap into those gifts, we may rediscover a considerable piece of our God-given identities. More importantly, we can express our gratitude to God for entrusting us with such gifts when He created us.

FINDING YOUR VISION

It's easy to talk about how essential vision is. What's tricky, however, is getting started finding yours. God has a vision for your life that's ideally suited to your skills and personality. Therefore, you must begin by surrendering entirely to Him.

You may be confused to learn that my first recommendation for finding God's vision for your life is to strive to rid your heart and mind of sin. It's not an exciting thought, but a mind and heart that is clear and free from the shame and guilt that often accompanies sin is one that is better positioned to hear from God.

A couple of years ago, Canadian forest fires were so intense that even those in New York City faced crimson-tinged smog that was difficult to drive or see through. Folks were advised to cover their faces when leaving the house and to stay indoors as much as possible.

When sin is still in your life, your relationship with God will likely feel like looking through smog. You'll look to Him for answers, comfort, and direction, but you won't be able to see Him clearly. There will be a hazy distance between you and your heavenly Father that will confuse your relationship.

If you confess your sins to Him, He will readily forgive you! The Bible says, "If we confess our sins, he is faithful and just and will forgive us our sins and purify us from all unrighteousness" (1 John 1:9). That is terrific news. When we admit that we've been angry, unforgiving, lustful, or selfish, we don't have to wonder if God will wait for us to prove we want to change. Instead, we can be confident that He forgives us. It's in the past. We are now pure and free to serve Him.

Striving to live morally also ties in closely with my role as a parent. Notice I say "strive" because no one is perfect. No matter how hard we try, we will still sin occasionally. While I've struggled with pornography throughout my life, I still make a choice everyday to pursue healthier activities. I don't want my children to follow the same destructive behavior by accidentally becoming exposed to my old sins. Satan likes to tell us that we are too far gone and that God can't use us anymore. That is never the case. Once you realize you've been down the wrong path, you can turn back right away. God is ready to help you.

Turning from sin is usually difficult at first. You may need to enlist the help of a prayer or accountability partner. However, the fruit of your good decision will reward you in time. My children are growing up faster than I could have imagined, and I don't want to waste my precious time with them.

In addition to working with God to clear your life of destructive habits, ask others to tell you what they think you'd be good at. For example, can they see you working with young people or organizing a charity event? Find out if there are any gifts you have that others may notice.

Beyond that, you'll need to develop the right skills. To restate Dr. Myles Munroe's wise words, "If you want to become a success, do not seek success. Seek to become a person of value, and the world will pay you to be yourself."[4] A critical part of discovering your vision is doing the hard work. Pitch in and do the tasks no one else wants to. Work to reach those who are difficult. Become an expert with a particular craft or knowledge type. Others will begin to recognize your value before long. The success you seek in your ministry or career will naturally follow.

---

4. Munroe, "The 5 Kingdom Keys For Business Success," 1:01:16 to 1:01:41, https://www.youtube.com/watch?v=muZ3_2esQuQ.

Of course, you'll want to go to God often before you choose a path. Make sure you pray about how and where He can use you. Read the Bible for ideas about how He has made successes of others in the past. These individuals, such as Gideon, David, and Joseph, are often from humble backgrounds. Their stories are inspiring, but they always involve wholehearted obedience to God. And don't be afraid to dream big! Ephesians says He can do "immeasurably more than all we ask or imagine, according to his power that is at work within us" (Ephesians 3:20).

KNOW YOUR SPIRITUAL GIFTS

God has granted each of us who follow Him with specific spiritual gifts. These are different from but related to our natural talents or personality types. We all have gifts that we can use to serve others in both Christian ministry and our professional lives. Before you commit to your vision, you've got to make sure it's in line with what you do best.

Romans 12:6-8 says,

[6] We have different gifts, according to the grace given to each of us. If your gift is prophesying, then prophesy in accordance with your faith; [7] if it is serving, then serve; if it is teaching, then teach; [8] if it is to encourage, then give encouragement; if it is giving, then give generously; if it is to lead, do it diligently; if it is to show mercy, do it cheerfully.

Some Christians are granted the gift of **service**, or helping those in need. You may be an empathetic person who notices the needs of others and has the resources to help. For example, you can supply free babysitting for a struggling family or do the taxes of an older person. Maybe you realize someone can't mow their lawn, or your Bible study needs a house to meet in. If you have the gift of service, you're willing to make your space, time, or money available.

Others have the gift of **prophecy**, meaning they can speak the Word of God to those who need it. For example, you may realize that someone is involved in sin and requires reproof. Or you may know that God is inspiring a group of believers to do something great. Or you may sense when an acquaintance needs comfort or prayer. Those gifted with prophecy have a unique ability to discern God's voice in modern times.

The gift of **teaching** is straightforward and comes naturally to some. You may be able to explain concepts in Bible stories clearly or instruct others in God's commands in an honest and empathetic way. If this is your gift, your church is looking for Bible study leaders, Sunday School teachers, and youth workers who can powerfully train the next generation of believers.

Next, some are granted the gift of **encouragement**. There are Christians who have a history of abuse or discouragement that leaves them hungry for someone who will build them up. Encouragers speak kindly to the strengths of those weaker in the faith. People who encourage are also essential when other Christians are going through losses or trials. These individuals are aching for someone to comfort them or say positive things about the future. The right words of encouragement will lift their spirits and motivate them. Encouragers are critical to the strength of any church.

Still others have the gift of **giving**. They have been blessed with time or financial resources that they can generously supply to others. If you have an abundance and are eager to share your gifts to make others' lives easier, you may have the gift of giving.

This passage also speaks of the gift of **leadership**. Your church's deacons, ministry board members, and pastors are these people. These leaders can guide others with grace while earning respect by setting a good example. If you are interested in leadership, you may want to begin by being mentored by an existing leader at your church. Watch how they shepherd other adults while being sensitive to their needs. Then, find ways to get involved and demonstrate your competence.

Finally, Romans 12 discusses the gift of **mercy**. When you see others stressed or overwhelmed, you are ready to provide comfort and empathy. When you are merciful, you avoid judging others. Instead, you look for ways to ease their soul's burdens, provide practical help, and be a source of strength.

BE ATTENTIVE

God's vision for your life will always maximize your spiritual gifts. It will also involve your natural talents and personality type, which we uncovered in the last chapter.

It's essential, however, to distinguish between God's vision and your notions. For example, you may hear of a need in youth ministry and immediately envision a weekly program with hundreds of spiritually seeking teens in attendance. However, you may not have the time or resources to facilitate something at this level.

Psalm 127:1 says, "Unless the Lord builds the house, the builders labor in vain. Unless the Lord watches over the city, the guards stand watch in vain." Simply put, if God isn't behind your vision, it will not succeed. The first checkbox for your vision is that it should be in line with His Word. Beyond that, you'll need to remember your other responsibilities and commitments. God does not want you to neglect these to chase a new dream, as they are also part of your ministry on earth. Your job and family are always involved in your vision.

More specifically, if you have an idea for a new ministry, business venture, or geographical move, you'll need to pray continually about it and discuss the matter often with other believers. You may, for example, have a close relationship with someone in your Bible study that you trust for good advice. Ask them, "Do you think this ministry would work in our church?" or, "Do you think I could make a career move like this right now?" If they seem positive about your idea, ask them for thoughts on how to make things work smoothly. You can also ask other believers to lift you in prayer.

Next, look for minor signs that you're on the right track. For example, others may tell you they have been looking for a ministry like the one you're considering starting. God sometimes speaks in more subtle ways when it's time for you to make a move.

Your vision will use your spiritual gifts, talents, and personality traits. God won't ask you to take on a task you aren't suited for.

QUESTIONS

1. What do you believe your spiritual gifts are, based on the passage from Romans we looked at?
2. How do you believe God wants to use those gifts in your life?
3. Is there a more extensive vision you've always wanted to discuss with other believers? What small steps can you take to begin bringing your dreams into focus?

CHAPTER 10

PREPARING FOR YOUR PURPOSE

God has been preparing you for your purpose for your entire life. Your talents, gifts, and experiences make you ideally suited for the work He has called you to. Still, coming into your specific purpose requires some training and planning. Preparation will lead to greater effectiveness and confidence.

GOD'S UNIVERSAL PURPOSE

It's important to distinguish between your calling and God's universal purpose for your life. He created man in His own image for a reason. Genesis 1:26-28 tells us that God said,

> 26 "Let us make mankind in our image, in our likeness, so that they may rule over the fish in the sea and the birds in the sky, over the livestock and all the wild animals, and over all the creatures that move along the ground."
>
> 27 So God created mankind in his own image,
> in the image of God he created them;
> male and female he created them.

74

28 God blessed them and said to them, "Be fruitful and increase in number; fill the earth and subdue it. Rule over the fish in the sea and the birds in the sky and over every living creature that moves on the ground."

God created humans to fill the earth with more people and rule over the animals, plants, and fish. Like our heavenly Father, we have sound minds and are called to lead with intelligence and compassion. Christian men must lead our families by setting a godly example. We shouldn't be afraid to stand up for what is right and to show mercy when it's called for. It's also our job to rule over creation responsibly. You can teach your family about caring for their property, pets, and food resources without being wasteful.

Furthermore, God calls us to be fruitful and multiply in number. Many people believe children to be a burden, especially when they are born when we aren't expecting them. Yet they are a blessing to us as we get older! They infuse our lives with youthful energy and plans for the future.

Psalm 127:4-5a says, "Like arrows in the hands of a warrior are children born in one's youth. Blessed is the man whose quiver is full of them." When we have children, we have strength, like a warrior does when he has a healthy supply of arrows. They provide us with comfort, hope, and meaning.

Christians have another universal purpose: spreading the good news of Jesus. In Matthew 28:19, He told us, "Therefore go and make disciples of all nations, baptizing them in the name of the Father and of the Son and of the Holy Spirit." There are many people who don't know Christ in your workplace, neighborhood, and kids' soccer club. While you may not be handing out tracts, you can show them His love through your kindness, goodness, and enthusiasm. Opportunities will come for you to mention your church or faith. Don't let these pass you by. Matthew 5:13-16 tells us,

[13] "You are the salt of the earth. But if the salt loses its saltiness, how can it be made salty again? It is no longer good for anything, except to be thrown out and trampled underfoot.

[14] "You are the light of the world. A town built on a hill cannot be hidden. [15] Neither do people light a lamp and put it under a bowl. Instead they put it on its stand, and it gives light to everyone in the house. [16] In the same way, let your light shine before others, that they may see your good deeds and glorify your Father in heaven."

God's people are the salt of the earth, called to season everything with goodness and honesty, keeping it holy and fresh. Others will look at you and realize you're the real thing: an imperfect person doing their best to live uprightly. We are also the world's light, pointing others to Jesus with our good deeds. In biblical times, when people had a light, such as an oil lamp, they would put it on a stand so everyone in a dark home could benefit. In the same way, we shouldn't just help others and keep it to ourselves. Let them see us showing mercy and giving to others. It will remind them of what is right in the world and point them to Him.

PREPARING FOR YOUR SPECIFIC PURPOSE

Beyond God's general purpose for your life, He also has a specific one: the occupation He has called you to and your ministry within the Church.

Once you've taken an honest look at your talents, personality, and spiritual gifting to determine your calling, you're ready to start preparing for it. Purpose cannot be fulfilled alone. It will be bigger than one person, especially if you want to leave a legacy. Your success will depend upon you having the right people in your corner.

Many people looking to start a ministry or transition careers enlist the help of a spiritual mentor. Find someone who is a Christian and is respected in your church and community. This individual might be working in a role similar to the one you'd like to get involved in, or they may run a successful business. A strong mentor will have encountered obstacles and setbacks that they rose above. You may have a supportive spouse and friend circle, but they might not have the specific knowledge and experience you require to accomplish your goal. The right mentor will provide you with fore-sight, wisdom, and encouragement that were grown in the soil of reality.

It may be tempting to select someone as a mentor simply because their line of work is similar. For example, maybe you want to start a men's ministry in your community, and you know someone in a neighboring town who has had great success with one. He may be someone you can go to for advice, but he might not be your perfect mentor. You'll want someone who believes in you, your dream, and your ability to bring your vision to fruition. Finding someone who will be honest when you need redirection is also essential.

You may have to find someone in a different ministry or profession than your own. If your missions have similar principles, you can get great support from your mentor. Try meeting biweekly for coffee to discuss your goals and progress. The right mentor will hold you accountable if you are off course and encourage you when you have small wins.

Another part of preparing for your purpose is educating yourself, which may mean reading up on your ministry or taking classes to help you develop knowledge and skills. These days, going back to "school" is easier than ever because you can learn online after the kids are in bed. You will have much more confidence in fulfilling your purpose if you fill your mind with knowledge daily.

As was the case with me, you may hold another job while planning to transition to a new venture. This can make educating yourself tricky, but not impossible. You can use your driving time to listen to podcasts or meet with a ministry expert during your lunch break. Making the most of every minute is critical to starting something new if you already have other responsibilities at home.

Preparing for your purpose may also involve flexibility. For example, you may have been determined to start a men's ministry at your church, only to find that many more men are interested in attending meetings with their wives. Or you may set out looking to transition into a career in marketing, only to discover a need for teachers in your area that you could quickly fill.

Be open to God's leading. If you encounter unexpected opportunities that align with your skills, personality, and family situation, you may want to pursue a slightly different direction than originally planned. God won't steer you wrong if you take the matter to Him through prayer, Scripture reading, and fellowship with His people.

If God has called you to a purpose, He won't leave you without the resources to accomplish it. The important thing is to seek out the answers for your life today, rather than worrying about what you may have missed out on yesterday.

IT'S NOT TOO LATE

Many people avoid exploring new ministries or professions in mid-life because they feel the time for such decisions is past them. The good news is that God knew all about your life's trajectory when He called you. He can use your background to make you an even stronger leader.

Do you remember the story about Moses and the burning bush we covered in chapter five? Many people hear this narrative and believe that Moses must have been in his twenties when he killed the Egyptian and a man of around forty when God called him to lead Israel out of captivity. Yet the truth is that Moses was around forty when he fled Pharaoh and eighty when God appeared to him in that fiery shrub!

God taught Moses a great deal during his time in the desert. He raised a family near his in-laws, which taught him some diplomacy and patience. Moses also became fully aware of his weaknesses and ready to depend on God, which was not the case when he was a well-educated young man living comfortably in Pharaoh's home.

You may have also heard the story of Abraham and Sarah. In Genesis 12:1-3, God promised Abraham that his descendants would be as numerous as the citizens of a nation. Yet, at eighty-five years old, Abraham still wondered where that baby was. His wife Sarah was well past child-bearing age and was probably ready to head to the desert retirement village for some camel bingo. She gave Abraham her slave, Hagar, to sleep with, and Hagar conceived (Genesis 16:1-4). This act of unbelief led to many problems for the family.

But despite this screw-up, God gave Abraham the promised child when he was 100 and Sara was 90. She became a "mother of all nations" (Genesis 17:16). God's plan will always manifest in His timing, not ours.

Joshua was the leader of Israel after Moses died. He came into his role at ninety years old, just twenty years before the end of his life. Joshua believed in God's power to fulfill His promise, even when almost everyone else said the enemy looked too intimidating to defeat (Numbers 14:6-10). Joshua became the leader who marched Israel into the Promised Land of Canaan.

The Apostle John was ninety-nine years old when he wrote the Book of Revelation. And Noah was six hundred years old when he built the ark!

Indeed, those who lived in ancient times often lived longer than modern men. Still, it's crucial to understand that the right time for your purpose is not when you think it should be, but when God determines it should happen. As with Moses, God will not back off when you start telling Him how unqualified you think you are. Instead, He will remind you that He is with you, and that is all you need.

QUESTIONS

1. What is God's general purpose for your life? What do you believe to be your specific purpose?
2. How can you begin preparing for your specific purpose this week?
3. Have you ever had to "tweak" your goals due to the available opportunities? How did this help you grow?
4. Have you ever wondered if you're too old to fulfill God's purpose for your life? How do you think being older (than some!) could be an advantage in what God has called you to do?

CHAPTER 11

THE HOLY SPIRIT: THE ULTIMATE BUSINESS PARTNER

Many people go into business with a partner to offset their financial risk and benefit from someone else's knowledge. In some cases, it's an intelligent decision. In others, disagreements over choices and fights over profits make folks wish they had ventured out independently.

But what if you had a partner in your professional life who could always encourage you? What if your associate already knew the future? What if that person was always right?

Many people love to consult others before undertaking a new adventure, yet few lean heavily on the Holy Spirit. If you've been saved, the Third Person of the Trinity lives in you. He is a beautiful resource for those looking to raise strong families and work honorably during our time on Earth.

JESUS COMFORTS

I was recently reading John 14, in which Jesus comforted His disciples about His impending departure from the world. The chapter has three critical sections.

DR. BRYAN L. MALONE, ACC

In the first section, Jesus comforted His disciples, telling them:

[1] "Do not let your hearts be troubled. You believe in God; believe also in me. [2] My Father's house has many rooms; if that were not so, would I have told you that I am going there to prepare a place for you? [3] And if I go and prepare a place for you, I will come back and take you to be with me so that you also may be where I am." (John 14:1-3)

Jesus was letting His disciples know He was going to Heaven to prepare homes for them. He wouldn't be physically present on Earth but would still be working on their behalf.

It's easy for us to become anxious, worried, fearful, and distracted. Jesus knew this and comforted His followers. How many foolish mistakes have we made because we were afraid or distraught? We could have been clear-headed if we focused on our Savior. He always knows the best way and will be with us even when we fail. The next time you're upset about a setback or financial problem, take your concerns to Him in prayer. The Holy Spirit will be there to provide guidance and consolation.

The second part of the chapter focuses on Jesus' oneness with the Father. He says, "Believe me when I say that I am in the Father and the Father is in me; or at least believe in the evidence of the works themselves" (John 14:11). So, Jesus *is* the Father in human form. He told His disciples they would find Him in Jesus when they sought God, as the two are one. Our relationship with Jesus gives us access to all three parts of the Trinity: the Father, Son, and Holy Spirit.

In John 14:12, He continues, "Very truly I tell you, whoever believes in me will do the works I have been doing, and they will do even greater things than these, because I am going to the Father." Jesus called us to do even greater works than Him, so our purpose must be significant in His eyes. This calling is not something we can imagine on our own. Instead, we must pray that He will reveal it and equip us to walk in it.

The last part of this chapter focuses on the Holy Spirit. Jesus loved us too much to leave us alone when He returned to the Father. Verses 16-18 say:

> [16] "And I will ask the Father, and he will give you another advocate to help you and be with you forever— [17] the Spirit of truth. The world cannot accept him, because it neither sees him nor knows him. But you know him, for he lives with you and will be in you. [18] I will not leave you as orphans; I will come to you." (John 14:16-18)

The Helper would not be someone that the world would recognize or accept. Have you ever wondered why non-believers don't seem bothered when someone is distressed or doing something unethical? That's because they don't have the Holy Spirit. He doesn't warn them or provide them with direction.

The Comforter brings solace and reminds us of what Jesus already told us. This includes His instructions on living life well, but it also involves our purpose. If Jesus has given your life a purpose, He will remind you of it. He will not leave you wondering how the work will be done.

Philippians 1:6 says you can be "confident of this, that he who began a good work in you will carry it on to completion until the day of Christ Jesus." God will not give you a purpose and then leave you helpless. He will give you what you need to finish the work and finish it well.

RECOGNIZING THE HOLY SPIRIT

Anyone who has been a believer for some time knows that several influences compete for our attention. Some of the promptings in your spirit come from your heavenly Father, but others are evil. Those in spiritual battles are often tempted to sin or hurt people out of spite. Still others of your impulses stem from your thoughts and imagination. They may be sins, but they could also be wrong decisions that seem suitable for worldly reasons.

One of the first barometers for recognizing the Holy Spirit's voice is checking whether your instinct aligns with God's Word. Will your venture make others' lives better? Will it encourage people to be generous or raise godly families? Is it pure, lovely, and admirable (Philippians 4:8)?

On the other hand, will it be easy to sin if you take on this new business or project? Will it require little white lies or an unfair distribution of profit? If you succeed, will others think more highly of Christians or less of them?

Similarly, the Holy Spirit will encourage you to help others. Scripture tells us, "And do not forget to do good and to share with others, for with such sacrifices God is pleased" (Hebrews 13:16). Maybe your business will bring affordable homes to young families or make investing more accessible for those without financial knowledge. Or perhaps you can provide free services for those who can't afford them with some of your earnings. When your business's ultimate goal is to serve, it will be successful.

It's essential, however, to note that God won't ask you to get involved in something you don't have the skills and resources to do well. When the Holy Spirit is in a project, it will make logical sense. This means you can speak to others in your church and community about it, and they will approve. They will believe you have a sound idea and agree that you are the right person to spearhead it.

Finally, God often speaks to us in soft, understated ways. The Holy Spirit is a gentleman Who won't shout at you or make you listen if you're not paying attention.

In 1 Kings, the prophet Elijah fled from Jezebel, who wanted to kill him. The Lord came to him and told him He would pass by.

[11] The Lord said, "Go out and stand on the mountain in the presence of the Lord, for the Lord is about to pass by."

Then a great and powerful wind tore the mountains apart and shattered the rocks before the Lord, but the Lord was not in the wind. After the wind there was an earthquake, but the Lord was not in the earthquake. [12] After the earthquake came a fire, but the Lord was not in the fire. And after the fire came a gentle whisper. [13] When Elijah heard it, he pulled his cloak over his face and went out and stood at the mouth of the cave.

Then a voice said to him, "What are you doing here, Elijah?" (1 Kings 19:11-13)

God can tear mountains apart with the wind, shake the earth, and start fires. He showed Elijah His strength before demonstrating His gentleness. The Lord spoke to Elijah in a whisper. When waiting to hear from God, don't merely heed the loudest noise you hear. Instead, listen for His soft, reasonable, holy prompting. You will hear Him when you seek Him with all your heart (Jeremiah 29:13).

PARTNERING WITH THE SPIRIT AND AVOIDING DISTRACTION

When you have a strong business partner, you will consult them often. When making a deal or an important decision, you'll immediately pick up the phone at their call. You need input and advice. You want to move forward knowing you have the backing of an expert.

The same is true when you're looking to walk with the Spirit. You need to pray often. Whenever you're worried or hopeful about something, you must go to Him. Others will have their opinions, and these can be valuable. However, it's important to value what God says above all.

If you want to walk in line with the Holy Spirit, you've got to make quiet time for Him every day, reading His Word, journaling, and searching your heart for sin. Some find it helpful to incorporate fasting or devotionals. Whatever you do, your time with the Lord should rejuvenate and purify you.

Distractions can easily cause your heart to become out of sync with the Spirit. You may be tempted to pick up your phone and scroll endlessly through social media to relax at the end of the day, but your spirit needs to connect with your Savior.

In Luke 4:1-13, Jesus faced temptation from Satan after fasting for forty days and forty nights. The enemy told Him, "If you are the Son of God, tell this stone to become bread" (Luke 4:3). It makes me wonder: Why would the enemy say something like that to Jesus if he knew Who He was? He wasn't looking for Jesus to prove His identity. He wanted to distract Him.

You could even argue that Satan was looking to kill Jesus right there by offering Him bread after a fast. If you know anything about fasting, you know that the human body wasn't designed to ingest bread after forty days and forty nights without food. The effects of the stomach attempting to break down solid bread once enzymes and acids have gone into a long rest period could be harmful, even fatal.

Remember, the enemy came to steal, kill, and DESTROY (John 10:10). The aim here was to stop Jesus' purpose (the plan of salvation) and keep it from moving forward. Distractions are one of the most dangerous barriers between us and our purpose. They are not often evident, because the Devil is crafty and can present things in small ways that frequently appear good. We can spend years pursuing a purpose we believe is correct, but it may have nothing to do with the real reason God placed us on Earth.

Some distractions are apparent. You know when you're spending too much time on X or getting sucked into an Internet rabbit hole of idle chatter or lewd content. Yet other things may not necessarily be destructive pursuits but simply waste your time. As we age, we become increasingly aware of how limited our time on earth really is.

The way Jesus responded to temptation in Luke 4 gives us the perfect way to handle distraction. First of all, He pointed back to God's Word. Jesus responded to Satan's offer of bread with, "It is written: 'Man shall not live on bread alone'" (Luke 4:4). Knowing

Scripture is a powerful way to counteract our propensity for distraction. The Bible calls God's Word "the sword of the Spirit" (Ephesians 6:17).

Many of us are busy and may feel that we don't have time to memorize Scripture. But you can commit to doing a bit of memorization, even if it's just one verse per week. These words of righteousness, encouragement, and victory can do much to counteract the enemy's attacks.

Secondly, Jesus could hold up what was presented to Him against the Word of God and immediately reject it. He was so immersed in God's teachings that He could clearly discern temptation for what it was. So it is with those of us who live Scripture-infused lives. We read the Bible, spend time with strong Christians, and listen only to input that would glorify Him. We can recognize sin immediately and push it out of the way.

Thirdly, Jesus was clear from the beginning about His purpose here on earth. He was here to reconcile all of humankind back to God. Thus, He was focused on His assignment and shunned anything that got in its way. He was in tune with the Father. Knowing your purpose can clarify things and clear your path in unique ways.

Furthermore, you must obey to ensure that you're walking with the Spirit daily. He has provided believers with a sensitivity to sin, and when your mind wanders into lust, greed, or anger, you won't feel right, making you ineffective as a leader and bringing you out of sync with the great Comforter. It may be difficult initially to retrain your mind to avoid sinful thoughts. Instead of chastising yourself, you can begin by replacing those images and ideas with other things. These could be ways to improve your finances, family, or church. Or you could simply admire God's creation. In time, your mind will default to more God-honoring thoughts when bored or at rest.

Finally, partnering with the Spirit means constantly cultivating the gifts He has blessed you with. These may be your natural talents, such as speaking, writing, or building. You should also be building your spiritual gifts, including serving, teaching, and encouraging.

You can work on these in church or during your leisure time. Keeping your life in step with the Spirit (Galatians 5:25) requires days spent on activities that please Him.

QUESTIONS

1. Why do you think the Holy Spirit was sent to comfort us? Who do you usually seek first when you need guidance and assurance? Why is the Holy Spirit a better resource?
2. What habits keep you from walking in tune with the Spirit? How can you arrange your schedule to bring you more in line with His will?
3. What distractions keep you from the Holy Spirit? How can you minimize their presence in your life?

CHAPTER 12

GETTING OFF THE GROUND

As a leadership coach, I often help folks create a roadmap for their specific purpose and assignment in life. As a Christian, I know that finding true meaning will involve discovering God's corporate and individual purposes for them. It helps when I ask questions like "What problems do you like to solve?" and "What is it that you're particularly passionate about?"

In my case, God gave me a vision to see my hometown of Memphis become a more progressive, economically healthy, and culturally diverse city. I learned that passion is critical, because there will always be times when you're tired and don't feel like pressing forward. During these moments, you've got to understand why you're doing what you're doing and keep working toward the goal. My personal experience has made me confident that helping others find their true calling is a God-ordained mission. This knowledge keeps me going when my gas tank is running low.

When clients want to discover their life's mission, I look at their dominant gifts, talents, traits, and personalities. I've got a person who needs help in front of me, and I try to place them in an area where they will be working as God intended. I ask myself, "How can I solve this problem through leadership coaching?"

My next step is to get busy on the assignment. You may not be looking for coaching clients; instead, you might search for students, a local church, or cleaning customers. Keep praying, asking around, and trying different places to find your mission field. God will be faithful in bringing you there.

HE THAT PLOWETH

One day, as I got up from praying, I heard 1 Corinthians 9:10: "Surely he says this for us, doesn't He? Yes, this was written for us, because whoever plows and threshes should be able to do so in the hope of sharing in the harvest." I wondered if it was God's voice or just some random thought, but I opened my Bible to read it. Then, I asked God the two questions I always ask before reading His Word: (1) "What does this mean?" and (2) "How does this relate to me discovering my identity and purpose?"

Sometimes, the connection between the verse and my situation is obvious. In this case, it wasn't, so I did some further analysis.

After reading the whole chapter, I realized it's about work in the Kingdom. I can expect to be rewarded and supported if I diligently fulfill my responsibilities. My labor will not be in vain if I operate within my purpose. I will eventually reap the fruit of my work.

Working in the Kingdom is all the more reason to reconnect intentionally with our identity and purpose. We must be in complete alignment with God's will for our lives. He tells us to seek His Kingdom first. Matthew 6:30-34 says,

> [30] "If that is how God clothes the grass of the field, which is here today and tomorrow is thrown into the fire, will he not much more clothe you—you of little faith? [31] So do not worry, saying, 'What shall we eat?' or 'What shall we drink?' or 'What shall we wear?' [32] For the pagans run after all these things, and your heavenly Father

knows that you need them. [33] But seek first His kingdom and His righteousness, and all these things will be given to you as well. [34] Therefore do not worry about tomorrow, for tomorrow will worry about itself. Each day has enough trouble of its own."

Jesus told us not to wake up every day and worry about dinner or how we'll afford clothes for work. He *knows* we need these things. Instead, we have to seek Him first. And if He is diligent and caring enough to ensure the birds on our cable lines have enough to drink and wear, how much more will He care for us?

We must seek God's Kingdom through prayer, Bible reading, and diligence in the work He sets before us. That will be the thing that sustains us in Christ.

STAYING HUNGRY

Every day, we are at the center of a critical spiritual battle. 2 Corinthians 10:3-5 says,

[3] For though we live in the world, we do not wage war as the world does. [4] The weapons we fight with are not the weapons of the world. On the contrary, they have the divine power to demolish strongholds. [5] We demolish arguments and every pretension that sets itself up against the knowledge of God, and we take captive every thought to make it obedient to Christ.

From the moment we awake, evil forces are looking to distract and discourage us. It's a constant struggle in my mind. I have to choose God daily, or the Enemy will win out.

My routine involves spending time with God every day and journaling. Yet it's so important that this doesn't become just another required exercise, something to check off my to-do list. When it comes to things like going to the gym, I don't have trouble getting going. That's because weightlifting and cardio have been a part of my routine since high school. For nearly thirty years, I have been physically active in at least some capacity. I'm used to the way it energizes me. In the same way, spending time with God has become an essential part of my routine. I must fight my spiritual battles and pull down strongholds. Complacency, distractions, and laziness tend to pull us away from God. His Word speaks about renewing our minds daily and not conforming to the ways of this world (Romans 12:2).

It's so easy to get "set in our ways." Even if we're young, we can conform to our culture. We'll let down our guard and let any type of thinking take root. If we don't stay grounded in Jesus, we will drift ashore like a boat without an anchor.

2 Corinthians 10:5 talks about demolishing every thought that exalts itself above God. What needs to be pulled down in your life? Is it TV, the Internet, or social media? Could it be the approval of a work supervisor or a romantic interest? Sometimes, it's the attitude that our quiet time with God is just another requirement on our daily task list rather than an engaging, deep, and meaningful time with Him.

As believers, we have the authority to bring these thoughts down. If we don't, we will simply go through the motions. Becoming the kind of Christian who is deeply embedded in God's Word and promises will not come without effort. It requires a daily capturing and redirecting of thoughts. Yet taking the time to do this will make you the person God intended you to be. We are only on this earth for a short time. Use it to create a life that glorifies Him.

QUESTIONS

1. What do you believe your mission field to be? Have you found a specific one yet? If not, how can you look for it?
2. What kinds of distractions and thoughts keep you from spending time with God? How can you pull these down?

CHAPTER 13
KEEPING SIGHT OF YOUR PURPOSE

In the King James Version of the Bible, Proverbs 28:3 says, "A poor man that oppresseth the poor is like a sweeping rain which leaveth no food."

When I first read that, I thought, "Who is the poor man? Why would he exploit or oppress someone lowly? Is he not lowly himself? Could it be that he does not know Jesus as Lord?"

As I began to research the verse, I realized that King Solomon was comparing the act of exploitation or oppression to the loss of a basic necessity. It's that bad. A sweeping rain would cause widespread flooding and the loss of an important crop, such as food.

This verse reflects the seriousness of taking advantage of people. To be *oppressed* is to be exploited or systematically harmed by others. Some believe this Proverb is about what happens when a formerly poor ruler forgets his humble origins and takes advantage of people once he has attained money, success, or power.

In the same way, we can lose our way in life. We can become so wrapped up in our own doing and getting that we forget our purpose and passion. We stop showing compassion and empathy. Because there is no vision or discipline, we throw off restraint (Proverbs 29:18) and take advantage of others.

One thing about reconnecting with our purpose and rediscovering who we are is that we have to come to a place where we fully understand the intentions of our Creator and the way He thinks. Once we realize how God approaches people, we can align our thoughts and make the proper adjustments. Since God created us in His image, our goal must be to take on the mindset of Christ. God does not desire that we take advantage of the poor, lowly, and less fortunate. Instead, we must protect and defend them (Proverbs 31:8-9, Luke 3:11).

Losing sight of your purpose can impact how you treat yourself and everyone else. Ask the Lord to renew your mind daily with His purpose for your life so that it remains at the top of your mind. Then, write it down so you can remind yourself again.

God's primary purpose for your life is so much more than what you do for a living or your role at church. He wants you to show compassion and grace and reach out to the hurting and brokenhearted. God needs you to show love and kindness to a world in desperate need, and He has given you everything you need to do that job.

TAKE DELIGHT IN THE LORD

The Bible says, "Take delight in the Lord, and he will give you the desires of your heart" (Psalm 37:4). If we genuinely desire to understand and reconnect with God, we must conform to His desires, not our worldly ones. Our purpose must be who He says we are, not what we think we should be. We must delight in His Word and holy things. Then, our hearts will be content with the blessings that follow.

God's Word also tells us not to worry about life's necessities but to acknowledge Him in all our ways. Then, He will smooth our paths (Proverbs 3:5-6) and remove obstacles in our way. Acknowledging

God in our ways means we will involve Him in everything we do. When we make decisions and interact with others, we will include Him. Including God does not just involve consulting His advice before doing whatever we please. Instead, we will seek His directions and guidance, following His ways first. This must be true even if what He says contradicts our natural desires.

The more we invite God into our lives, the clearer His purpose will become. We must prioritize His thoughts, directions, and ways.

WHATEVER IS PURE

Let me give you an example of how we can abuse purpose. I can recall being exposed to sex at a very young age, primarily through movies my older brother would watch (HBO and Cinemax Friday After Dark) and the magazines he kept. Also, as an eight-year-old, I would often sneak into my stepfather's closet to look at his secret stash of pornographic videos, until one day, I got caught.

In my adolescent years, I listened to older friends who were experimenting with sex. It seemed that to be accepted, I needed to know what it was like to experience sex and have my own stories to tell. I feared being ridiculed by being called "the virgin"—as if that were some sort of badge of shame.

As a teenager, I didn't understand God's true intention for sex to be within the covenant of marriage. Nor was I taught early on to value my body as a temple of the Holy Spirit. So, I did what most young, hormone-raged boys end up doing. I experimented with sex for the first time at age fourteen and continued to abuse it throughout my teenage and young adult life, racking up partners like they were notches on my belt. Not to mention, I had developed an unhealthy addiction to pornography.

It wasn't until I was able to go to God as an adult, having established somewhat of a decent relationship with Him, that I began to truly understand His purpose for sex: to be fruitful and multiply within the safe boundaries of matrimony. Had I been taught this early in my life, my entire perspective on sex and relationships could have been shaped more healthily.

APPROVAL ADDICTION

You may be seeking meaning, not in sex, but in the approval of others. This will ultimately lead to low self-worth, no confidence, and a lack of self-esteem, because others won't constantly affirm us. There will be times when to do the right thing, you will disagree with those you love and have to make decisions without their stamp of approval. Conversely, you may end up going along with things you don't want if you are living in the prison of people-pleasing. Remember chapter five: FOPO is a killer of purpose.

Whenever we don't understand the purpose of something, we are bound to abuse it. To find a genuinely satisfying purpose for our lives, we must go to the One Who created us.

God's overall purpose for your life is that you love, enjoy, and serve Him. Staying the course requires a strong group of fellow believers, a daily routine of prayer and Bible reading, and good Christian supplemental material. Saturate yourself in the Word. That way, even when you stumble, you can get back on track, since your mind will be pure.

Scripture tells us, "Finally, brothers and sisters, whatever is true, whatever is noble, whatever is right, whatever is pure, whatever is lovely, whatever is admirable—if anything is excellent or praise-worthy—think about such things" (Philippians 4:8). We all know the impure things our minds would dwell on if we allowed them to. But what God-sanctioned things provide you with an immediate boost? Do you enjoy praise music, working out at the gym, or a run through the park? Are there Christian fiction books you can't put down?

When your mind is full of things that honor God and serve Him, you won't be distracted by thoughts that will bring you shame and disappointment. You may need to stay away from your computer or phone during downtime. Instead, choose a path leading to a sharper mind, stronger body, and better witness. You will achieve those things you set out to do when you first started following God.

GOALS AND MORE GOALS

When it comes to God's specific purpose for your life, you'll need to write down your goals. This will help you stay on track and avoid making decisions that will distract you.

Long-term goals are those ultimate things you want to do in your career and ministry. For example, you might hope to get promoted to management at work or start an evangelism website that reaches people overseas. These are lovely dreams that will keep you motivated and future-minded.

Short-term goals are the day-by-day and month-by-month baby steps that will get you where you'd love to be in five or ten years. For example, you may want to close a certain number of sales this week or be leading a successful Bible study for men in your age group by the end of the month.

SMART Goals are those that are Specific, Measurable, Attainable, Relevant, and Time-Bound.[1] Writing your goals down regularly will help you stay focused on the specific purpose God has for your life. When you have goals to meet every day, you won't have time to waste on sinful thoughts and practices.

The first aim of your goal is that it should be Specific. So, you won't want to write, "Start a small Bible study." Instead, you could say, "Have a Bible study that meets three times a month, with at least five regular members." This level of detail helps you clearly define what success will look like. It can also help you meet your goal quickly, boosting your confidence.

---

1. Mark Stibich, "How to Set SMART Goals: A Template to Help Clarify Your Mental Health Goals," Verywell Mind, January 1, 2024, https://www.verywellmind.com/smart-goals-for-lifestyle-change-2224097

The second aspect of your goal should be that it is Measurable. You can measure attendance every week to ensure that you have a certain number of people attending your Bible study. If you exceed that number, your group is growing even faster than you planned, and you can adjust your goal accordingly.

Third, your goal needs to be Attainable. For example, if your church has only fifty people, it's unlikely that your Bible study will exceed that number. Don't waste your time on goals that you probably won't be able to reach, which will only discourage you. Instead, be realistic, and you will likely exceed your goals.

Next, your goal should be Relevant. You don't want an aim that isn't honoring God. Your goal shouldn't be, "I want to make a lot of money this week so I can blow it on a great weekend with the guys." Instead, make sure it is something that will benefit you and others.

Finally, your goal has to be Time-Bound. That means that you should plan to reach it within a specific frame of time. Again, think realistically. Starting a Bible study with a few members after three months is a reasonable goal. Growing it to twice that size might be doable within a year, and multiplying it further is something you could aim for over several years.

Once you're focused on short- and long-term goals, your mind will align with God's specific purposes for you, keeping you busy and giving sin little chance to grow in your heart.

QUESTIONS:

1. What are some long- and short-term goals that you have? Are any of these SMART goals? How can you use the SMART model to create goals you can meet over the next few months?
2. What habits do you know will lead to sin and temptation? How can you replace them with more God-honoring activities?

3. Are there times when you become self-absorbed and
   forget about the needs of others? How can you redirect
   your focus?

CHAPTER 14
JOSEPH AND PURPOSE

Tf your life is like mine, it's been a mixture of good and bad breaks. One of the most challenging things to overcome is when others deliberately set out to harm you, motivated by jealousy or hatred. It's easy to think "How could God let that happen? I was trying to do the right thing," or "Does He even see what's going on?"

The good news is that God sees everything, even the intentions of others' hearts that you don't know about. He is the ultimate purveyor of justice. Throughout your journey, you may be shocked by the road's direction. You must remain steadfast in faith, trusting that God's purpose for your life will prevail.

A COAT OF MANY COLORS

If you know anything about Joseph, it probably concerns his vivid coat. Joseph was the first-born son of Jacob's wife, Rachel, whom he loved deeply. Before Joseph's arrival, Jacob had six sons with Leah, Rachel's sister. Jacob did not love Leah, but Laban—Rachel and Leah's father—tricked Jacob into marrying Leah before being given

Rachel as a bride. God had compassion for Leah and allowed her to bear Jacob's sons (Genesis 29:31). He also had children with the handmaids of both Leah and Rachel. Jacob gave his beloved son Joseph a gorgeous coat in an array of colors as a token of how much he valued him:

> [3] Now Israel loved Joseph more than any of his other sons, because he had been born to him in his old age; and he made an ornate robe for him. [4] When his brothers saw that their father loved him more than any of them, they hated him and could not speak a kind word to him.
>
> [5] Joseph had a dream, and when he told it to his brothers, they hated him all the more. [6] He said to them, "Listen to this dream I had: [7] We were binding sheaves of grain out in the field when suddenly my sheaf rose and stood upright, while your sheaves gathered around mine and bowed down to it."
>
> [8] His brothers said to him, "Do you intend to reign over us? Will you actually rule us?" And they hated him all the more because of his dream and what he had said. (Genesis 37:3-8)

Joseph's brothers were so jealous they couldn't even be kind to him. Have you met someone at work or in your family who couldn't speak nicely to you? You might feel the hurt deeply, but it didn't go unnoticed by God.

Joseph did not help himself by telling his brothers about his dream, in which his brothers' sheaves of grain bowed down to his own. His brothers hated him even more when they realized he'd had a premonition about ruling over them.

That was just the beginning of Joseph's misfortunes. Later in the chapter, his brothers took out their revenge:

> [17b] So Joseph went after his brothers and found them near Dothan.
>
> [18] But they saw him in the distance, and before he reached them, they plotted to kill him.

[19] "Here comes that dreamer!" they said to each other. [20] "Come now, let's kill him and throw him into one of these cisterns and say that a ferocious animal devoured him. Then we'll see what comes of his dreams."

[21] When Reuben heard this, he tried to rescue him from their hands. "Let's not take his life," he said. [22] "Don't shed any blood. Throw him into this cistern here in the wilderness, but don't lay a hand on him." Reuben said this to rescue him from them and take him back to his father.

[23] So when Joseph came to his brothers, they stripped him of his robe—the ornate robe he was wearing— [24] and they took him and threw him into the cistern. The cistern was empty; there was no water in it.

[25] As they sat down to eat their meal, they looked up and saw a caravan of Ishmaelites coming from Gilead. Their camels were loaded with spices, balm and myrrh, and they were on their way to take them down to Egypt.

[26] Judah said to his brothers, "What will we gain if we kill our brother and cover up his blood? [27] Come, let's sell him to the Ishmaelites and not lay our hands on him; after all, he is our brother, our own flesh and blood." His brothers agreed.

[28] So when the Midianite merchants came by, his brothers pulled Joseph up out of the cistern and sold him for twenty shekels of silver to the Ishmaelites, who took him to Egypt. (Genesis 37:17b-28)

Isn't it interesting to see what his brothers hated about Joseph? They said, "Here comes the dreamer; let's see what happens to his dreams now" (verses 20-21). In this life, you will meet people who will hate you simply because you have big dreams. God has given you a vision and a purpose. Others will seek to snatch that from you if it's important enough. It's critical to keep your eyes on heaven and ignore your critics once you're confident you're on the right path.

Joseph's brothers spared his life due to the guilt of one of the brothers, and they sold him into slavery. Yet that was far from the end of his problems.

Joseph was brought into the service of Potiphar, a captain of the guard. God was with him and gave him success (Genesis 39:3). It's important to note that, ultimately, your success is up to God. His power can sustain you (Romans 14:4).

Moreover, God blessed Potiphar's house because of Joseph.

> ⁵ From the time he put him in charge of his household and of all that he owned, the Lord blessed the household of the Egyptian because of Joseph. The blessing of the Lord was on everything Potiphar had, both in the house and in the field. ⁶ So Potiphar left everything he had in Joseph's care; with Joseph in charge, he did not concern himself with anything except the food he ate. (Genesis 39:5-6b)

It's possible to be so blessed by God that even the unbelievers around you prosper due to your faithfulness. God blessed everything Potiphar owned, and he was content to leave everything in Joseph's hands.

As with the rest of Joseph's story, trouble wasn't far behind. Potiphar's wife was also impressed by Joseph, but in a different way. She asked him to sleep with her, but he refused (Genesis 39:7-10). She responded by accusing him of rape, and he was thrown in prison (Genesis 39:19-20). Yet even there,

> ²¹ The Lord was with him; he showed him kindness and granted him favor in the eyes of the prison warden. ²² So the warden put Joseph in charge of all those held in the prison, and he was made responsible for all that was done there. ²³ The warden paid no attention to anything under Joseph's care, because the Lord was with Joseph and gave him success in whatever he did. (Genesis 39:21-23)

It seemed that, no matter how many people falsely accused

Joseph, God continued to bless him. Even in prison, he was promoted to a position of leadership! God granted him success and the unshakable trust of the prison warden.

DREAMING ON

While Joseph was in prison, he had some company. Pharaoh threw a cupbearer and a baker there. Both were discouraged because they had dramatic dreams but couldn't interpret them.

Joseph, however, had the gift of prophecy and could interpret them (Genesis 40:1-22). The cupbearer, whose future turned out favorably, was restored to Pharaoh's service, but he forgot about Joseph and did not mention him to Pharaoh as Joseph had asked (Genesis 40:23).

Joseph thought he was getting a chance at restoration, but the opportunity was lost. This is so important to remember when you're working toward your purpose. Sometimes, you think you've broken through, but God will ask you to wait a little longer. You must continue in faith until the time is right.

Finally, Joseph was placed in a position to understand why God had allowed him to be so abused and falsely accused by others. The Pharaoh had a dream and learned that a man in prison named Joseph could interpret them (Genesis 41:8-13). Joseph changed his clothes, shaved, took a break from his dungeon food, and went to see Pharaoh (Genesis 41:14). Pharaoh told Joseph about his dreams:

> [15] Pharaoh told Joseph, "I had a dream, and no one can interpret it. But I have heard it said of you that when you hear a dream you can interpret it."
>
> [16] "I cannot do it," Joseph replied to Pharaoh, "but God will give Pharaoh the answer he desires."
>
> [17] Then Pharaoh said to Joseph, "In my dream I was standing on the bank of the Nile, [18] when out of the river there came up seven cows, fat and sleek, and they grazed among the reeds. [19] After them,

seven other cows came up—scrawny and very ugly and lean. I had never seen such ugly cows in all the land of Egypt. ²⁰ The lean, ugly cows ate up the seven fat cows that came up first. ²¹ But even after they ate them, no one could tell that they had done so; they looked just as ugly as before. Then I woke up.

²² "In my dream I saw seven heads of grain, full and good, growing on a single stalk. ²³ After them, seven other heads sprouted —withered and thin and scorched by the east wind. ²⁴ The thin heads of grain swallowed up the seven good heads. I told this to the magicians, but none of them could explain it to me."

²⁵ Then Joseph said to Pharaoh, "The dreams of Pharaoh are one and the same. God has revealed to Pharaoh what he is about to do. ²⁶ The seven good cows are seven years, and the seven good heads of grain are seven years; it is one and the same dream. ²⁷ The seven lean, ugly cows that came up afterward are seven years, and so are the seven worthless heads of grain scorched by the east wind: They are seven years of famine.

²⁸ "It is just as I said to Pharaoh: God has shown Pharaoh what he is about to do. ²⁹ Seven years of great abundance are coming throughout the land of Egypt, ³⁰ but seven years of famine will follow them. Then all the abundance in Egypt will be forgotten, and the famine will ravage the land. ³¹ The abundance in the land will not be remembered, because the famine that follows it will be so severe. ³² The reason the dream was given to Pharaoh in two forms is that the matter has been firmly decided by God, and God will do it soon.

³³ "And now let Pharaoh look for a discerning and wise man and put him in charge of the land of Egypt. ³⁴ Let Pharaoh appoint commissioners over the land to take a fifth of the harvest of Egypt during the seven years of abundance. ³⁵ They should collect all the food of these good years that are coming and store up the grain under the authority of Pharaoh, to be kept in the cities for food. ³⁶ This food should be held in reserve for the country, to be used during the seven years of famine that will come upon Egypt, so

that the country may not be ruined by the famine." (Genesis 41:15-36)

Pharaoh's dreams plagued him, but luckily, Joseph did what responsible Christian men are called to do. Joseph interpreted the situation as God enabled him (verses 25-31), and he devised a practical solution (verses 33-36). There would be a famine, and Pharaoh should prepare for it by storing food during the seven years of abundance that would precede it (verses 35-36).

As a result of this interpretation, Joseph was in charge of all of Egypt at the ripe old age of thirty (Genesis 41:41-46). He stored grain for seven years, so Egypt was prepared when the famine arrived as prophesied (Genesis 41:56).

And who arrived in Egypt to purchase grain? It was the very brothers that had sold Joseph into slavery over two decades before!

Joseph did not reveal himself initially but sent his brothers back home twice to retrieve his full brother, Benjamin, and his father, Jacob. Eventually, he embraced his family and showered blessings on them, saying, "You intended to harm me, but God intended it for good to accomplish what is now being done, the saving of many lives." (Genesis 50:20).

WHAT IS NOW BEING DONE

Joseph's brothers had no good intentions when they sold him into slavery. They wanted him out of their lives forever. Moreover, Potiphar's wife sought Joseph's destruction and not his promotion.

However, God had other plans. All of the sabotage and misfortune Joseph endured as a young man brought him to a place of leadership in middle age. He was well respected and fit to bless others, including those who had sought his demise.

God does not abandon us when He allows us to face adverse conditions. He calls us to trust Him even more. He wants us to be a part of "what is now being done, the saving of many lives." Joseph could have opted to wallow in self-pity. Instead, he chose faith. Because of Joseph's faithfulness, God used his gifts, experiences, and personality to save those who needed Him and could not have been reached otherwise.

What pits and prisons have you faced along the way? God can use those situations to sharpen your mind, hone your compassion, and make you better able to reach the lost. Others may mean you harm, but He intends good. Don't lose sight of that. God has a purpose for your life that will ultimately rule the day.

Wherever you are today, God can use your failures, setbacks, and sins to turn you into the kind of servant used in unique places. Start your journey of figuring out how your background, talents, personality, and experiences can help you do His work on earth. The result will be a legacy you can be proud to pass along to the next generation.

QUESTIONS

1. How do you think Joseph was able to sustain his faith when he was thrown into prison and falsely accused of rape? How do you hang on to God during difficult times?
2. Why do you think God allowed Joseph to endure such pain before bringing him into a position of leadership?
3. Why do you think God allows adversity in your life? How did it help prepare you for what is now happening?

CONCLUSION

By now, you should understand how important it is to look to our Creator to understand our true identity and purpose, why He created us, and His definition of who we are. Once we can understand who we are from our Creator's perspective, we can then take steps to understand our individual makeups, discovering various strengths, gifts, and talents that can be used to fulfill our God-given and particular purposes.

Throughout this book, I have illustrated various real-life struggles that people (Christian men in particular) face as we reach the middle of our lives and begin to question whether or not we are where we are supposed to be. Life's challenges often leave us ruminating and analyzing until we hardly know whether we're coming or going! We lose focus and need reminding of who we indeed are. As you search for your identity and purpose, use this book, which provides practical action steps based on my experiences, as a guidebook. Answer the questions at the end of each chapter, do the exercises I suggest, and self-evaluate. Don't miss this opportunity to reconnect with your authentic self and move closer to fulfilling your purpose, because this book is just the beginning of what God has in store.

BIBLIOGRAPHY

"The 16 MBTI® Personality Types." Myers and Briggs Foundation. Accessed August 5, 2024. https://www.myersbriggs.org/my-mbti-personality-type/the-16-mbti-personality-types/.

Block, Melissa. "How the Myers-Briggs Personality Test Began in a Mother's Living Room Lab." NPR, September 22, 2018. https://www.npr.org/2018/09/22/650019038/how-the-myers-briggs-personality-test-began-in-a-mothers-living-room-lab.

"Disc Assessment." Wikipedia, July 25, 2024. https://en.wikipedia.org/wiki/DISC_assessment.

"Forgiveness: Letting Go of Grudges and Bitterness." Mayo Clinic, November 22, 2022. https://www.mayoclinic.org/healthy-lifestyle/adult-health/in-depth/forgiveness/art-20047692.

Franklin, Jentezen. "Love Like You've Never Been Hurt." Jentezen Franklin (Blog), April 13, 2018. https://jentezenfranklin.org/blog/love-like-youve-never-been-hurt/.

"Health Effects of Social Isolation and Loneliness." Centers for Disease Control and Prevention, March 26, 2024. https://www.cdc.gov/social-connectedness/risk-factors/index.html.

"How Happiness Affects Health." www.heart.org, May 20, 2020. https://www.heart.org/en/university-hospitals-harrington-heart-and-vascular/how-happiness-affects-health.

Martino, Jessica, Jennifer Pegg, and Elizabeth Pegg Frates. "The Connection Prescription: Using the Power of Social Interactions and the Deep Desire for Connectedness to Empower Health and Wellness." *American Journal of Lifestyle Medicine* 11, no. 6 (October 7, 2015): 466–75. https://doi.org/10.1177/1559827615608788.

Munroe, Myles. "Chasing Your Dream by Dr. Myles Munroe." Pneuma Tv. March 28, 2019. Youtube video, 21:20. https://www.youtube.com/watch?v=Ye1NJBZroVk.

Munroe, Myles. "The 5 Kingdom Keys For Business Success | Dr. Myles Munroe." Munroe Global. May 2, 2021. Youtube video, 1:13:43. https://www.youtube.com/watch?v=muZ3_2esQuQ.

Murthy, Vivek. "Work and the Loneliness Epidemic," Harvard Business Review, September 26, 2017, https://hbr.org/2017/09/work-and-the-loneliness-epidemic.

Perissinotto, Carla M., Irena Stijacic Cenzer, and Kenneth E. Covinsky. "Loneliness in Older Persons: A Predictor of Functional Decline and Death." *Archives of Internal Medicine* 172, no. 14 (July 23, 2012). https://doi.org/10.1001/archinternmed.2012.1993.

Regan, Sarah. "7 Signs You May Be An Ambivert & How To Thrive, From Personality Experts." mindbodygreen, June 30, 2022. https://www.mindbodygreen.com/arti

cles/ambivert-meaning-and-signs#:~:text=What%20is%20an%20am-bivert%3F,have%20no%20trouble%20with%20either.

Roth, Sam. "Social Isolation, Loneliness Increase Risk for Heart Failure." American College of Cardiology, February 1, 2023. https://www.acc.org/About-ACC/Press-Releases/2023/02/01/21/26/Social-Isolation-Loneliness-Increase-Risk-for-Heart-Failure#:~:text=The%20researchers%20found%20that%20both,loneliness%20was%20not%20also%20present.

Seidman, Gwendolyn. "How Do Digital and In-Person Interactions Affect Wellbeing?" Psychology Today, September 6, 2022. https://www.psychologytoday.com/us/blog/close-encounters/202209/how-do-digital-and-in-person-interactions-affect-wellbeing.

Seppälä, Emma. "Connectedness & Health: The Science of Social Connection." The Center for Compassion and Altruism Research and Education, May 8, 2014. https://ccare.stanford.edu/uncategorized/connectedness-health-the-science-of-social-connection-infographic/.

Stibich, Mark. "How to Set SMART Goals: A Template to Help Clarify Your Mental Health Goals." Verywell Mind, January 1, 2024. https://www.verywellmind.com/smart-goals-for-lifestyle-change-2224097.

ABOUT THE AUTHOR

Dr. Bryan Malone, ACC, CEO, and Founder of MGE Professional Coaching, LLC, is passionate about helping individuals become the best versions of themselves. He is an ICF-credentialed coach specializing in leadership coaching. Launched in 2019, MGE Professional Coaching, LLC offers coaching to high potentials, entry-level and mid-level management, and start-up entrepreneurs, as well as leadership training and keynote speaking services. His coaching philosophy centers around the idea that every client is capable and resourceful in discovering the solution that will take them from where they are now to where they want to be. Bryan has been featured in publications such as Memphis Voyager Magazine and the Memphis Business Journal, has been interviewed on WMC TV5's popular news segment "Bluff City Life," and has collaborated with esteemed partners such as Mid-South Executive Housing LLC and Nashville-based Black Business Boom. When not coaching personal clients, Bryan serves as a FedEx program manager and leadership facilitator, with over twenty years of corporate and leadership experience. He also serves as an adjunct instructor at the University of Memphis, teaching HR management, employment law, and employee relations courses. He and his wife, Natasha, have been married for eighteen years. They have four children: Tyler, Morgan, Daniel, and Penelope.

facebook.com/mgeprofessionalcoaching

x.com/MgeCoaching

instagram.com/mgecoaching

linkedin.com/company/mge-professional-coaching-llc

www.ingramcontent.com/pod-product-compliance
Lightning Source LLC
Chambersburg PA
CBHW070725130626
46553CB00005B/2156